David Swinstead Britton

A Selection of Poems, Paintings and Articles

Published by Leiston Press

Published Leiston Press, Unit 1B, Masterlord Industrial Estate, Leiston, Suffolk IP16 4XS and distributed by

David Britton

35, Churchfields

West Mersea

CO5 8QJ

ISBN 978 0 9554725 7 2

Design jjdoyle.com

Typeset by Doyle & Co, West Mersea

Printed and bound by Leiston Press, Leiston, Suffolk

David Swinstead Britton

David Swinstead Britton was born on 1 November 1937. His is related to a line of Swinsteads, which included, in Victorian times, a number of artists and musicians, including those Swinsteads who set up Hornsey Art College.

David was educated at Colchester Royal Grammar School and at New College, Oxford, graduating with an Honours Degree in History. He works as poet and painter and writer of stories, and of religious philosophy, partly from a traditional Quaker point of view (he has contributed articles to the Philosophical Journals *Theoria to Theory*, *Radical Philosophy*, *Quaker Theology Proceedings* and *Appraisal*).

As a poet, David won First Prize in 1977 for the Ver Poets Open Competition and also won First Prize in 1995 in the Suffolk Poetry Competition. His work has been shortlisted thirteen times in national and international competitions. *The Grove of Hollies* was published in 1980 by Essex University Press, and since then he has had some fifty poems and articles on poetry and painting published in a dozen or so small magazines. Has also devised and presented several programmes of poetry and music, performing at the Netherbow Theatre in Edinburgh, Tintagel House and the Merlin Theatre in Sheffield, the Headgate Theatre in Colchester and the Mercury Theatre Bar in Colchester, as well as at Quaker Meeting Houses in Colchester, Sudbury, Bury St Edmunds and Sheffield. David also performed at The Minories in Colchester and at other locations for the Colchester Literary Society.

As a painter, David held his first one-man exhibition at Project B Gallery, Colchester in 1975 and has had some twenty joint and mixed exhibitions since then, including at the Falcon Gallery in Boxford, the Chappel Gallery, the John Russell Gallery in Ipswich, and the Buckenham Gallery Southwold. He mounted a one-man exhibition at The Minories, Colchester in 1985, and a large exhibition at the Woodgates Gallery, East Bergholt in 1995. David was one of the Aldeburgh Festival Artists at the Cinema Gallery, Aldeburgh in 2002 and has exhibited more recently at Colchester's St Botolph's Festival. Three of his large paintings were bought for Colchester District Hospital in 1983, and many others hang in offices in London.

Acknowledgements

Chiefly to Anne Price Owen and the *David Jones Journal*, for several poems in this book first published there, and for the long piece 'Poetic Inspiration and Metaphysical Knowledge'.

Also to *Candelabrum*, for publishing some of the poems in here, and for their enthusiastic reception of my work at its first submission.

Also to *Other Poetry* for 'Cezanne's Mountain'.

Also to *Konnect* and to *Poetry Monthly*.

Also to *Mandeville Press*, many years ago, for 'The Country Soldier'.

Also to the Swedenborg Society for the poem 'Waiting' and the article 'Mystical Sabbath and Heavenly Work'.

Also to the Quaker Fellowship of Afterlife Studies and *Quaker Monthly* for 'A Moral Argument for Immortality'.

Also to *Appraisal* for 'Poetic Inspiration and Metaphysical Knowledge'.

Also to Linda Miller for her support for my work over many years, and her careful reading, appreciation and exposition in her article here included.

Contents

PAINTINGS

ARTICLES

Introduction

Born in Bishop's Stortford, and brought up mainly in Colchester, it was at the age of twelve, in the hot arid Eritrean landscape where he lived for a year, that David Britton started painting.

'There wasn't a suitable school and I spent all my time playing football and cricket, until I injured my knees, and went into hospital, and into plaster. Out of plaster, the injury hadn't healed, and to keep me occupied my father introduced me to an Italian painter who showed me how oils were done, and later to an English painter out there, who gave me advice and encouragement, and whom I used to watch at work in his studio. His name was Blake!'

Britton confesses it was a terrific nostalgia for England – driving him to copy photos of green landscapes with elm trees and Essex barns – which inspired his early work.

'I was a slow learner, and all the pieces I did, for about fifteen years, in those on-off days, had to be painted over, they were so awful! In my late teens and early twenties I used to cheer myself up by thinking about Cezanne, whose work I loved the most at that time, but who didn't produce anything worthwhile till the age of 35. Strangely, it was at precisely that age, in October 1973, that I produced the first work I was satisfied with – a little study of the Box Valley near Stoke by Nayland, done on the spot in about two hours on a lovely serene day. I had been working on the spot at every opportunity for some six months, on the good advice of a Mr Borrett, who owned Briggs' Book and Art Shop in Colchester's Crouch Street at that time. I'm sure it was the secret of the breakthrough I made. I'd asked Mr Borrett what was the point of outdoor work, and he said, without hesitation, "Truth of light." He was absolutely right, and I owe him a debt of gratitude.'

As for the poetry, it wasn't until his late twenties that Britton started writing. He gave up his teaching job in 1970, in order to write poetry. 'It felt like now or never for me. I had to take this risk, to give myself the precious untainted time that full-time teaching never seems to give. The pressure to create poetry was enormous, and I needed the time in which to roam the countryside, and to do nothing for days on end sometimes. In order to "do", one also has to "not do", and modern life steals those opportunities. It surely says something about the unrelenting demands of teaching, that I found it easier to be a house father to my two young children, to shop and cook and clean (this latter, up to a point, admittedly), and yet to find time and energy to paint out doors, than to be teaching, and using the weekends and some of the so-called 'long holidays'. I would never have written my main poems had I remained a teacher of History.'

Britton is never without a notebook, with its shopping at one end and poetry at the other. He writes ideas down in raw non-poetic form as they occur. Like the paintings, his poems link the mystical with a response to the natural world, and vary from the concrete and sensual to those he describes as the 'withdrawn type', which take off into the infinite.

'When I have finished two or three of these latter paintings, I find I am drawn back again to the solid and near-at-hand. It is as though the sense of vivid colour is re-born out of my occasional success in transcending it. I go from void to solid, and back to the void, as the rhythm of my life dictates. There is no formula for producing the large mystical paintings. They come if I am faithful and patient. I try to explore these realities in my poem "Butterfly in March Sunshine".

'I utterly refuse to be cowed by the political pressures in the various Arts Worlds, where phoneys and time-servers abound, into doing the kind of work that is found acceptable and "relevant". There are legions who say one "can't", these days, write a poem about a summer morning, or paint a picture of an Essex barn. These people have to be ignored, and in any case they will all be forgotten, every one of them! When I won First Prize in the Suffolk Poetry Competition for a poem called, precisely, "Summer Morning", the Judge who awarded me the Prize told me: "You were lucky to have me as a judge! I know hardly anyone else who would understand or appreciate what you are doing." She was right, as I had known for years anyway, and she was no bumpkin, though in the eyes of the self-styled promoters at the "cutting edge", people like us are all bumpkins. And Victor Hugo was a bumpkin – and yet is also the greatest French poet, as Andre Gide was forced to concede, with a rueful "Helas"!

'People who pride themselves on being at the "cutting edge" would do well to remind themselves of two things. Firstly, and especially in the realm of poetry, correct attitudes, even if worthy and ethical, do not necessarily produce good poetry. And neither does "relevance", or the nonsensical "reflecting the age in which we live". I explore this attitudinising in my article "The Poetry of Postures". Even the trendies know this is true, but in practice they will be enormously indulgent to work with the "correct" attitudes, while putting on their strictest critical hats in the face of a piece of work which ignores those attitudes, and goes its own unfashionable way.

'Secondly, there is a "cutting edge" far more important than that of artistic fashions, and it is the spiritual one that, in Ivor Gurney's memorable phrase "cuts falsehood like a knife". This knife may take longer to do its work, and is invisible to many of the people who make the running in our current establishments, but it cuts in the end, and is ruthless to bubble reputations and pushy types, and to that sense of being "in the swim", which seems to be so important to people of that kind. It is terrifying, because when these falsehoods are cut away, there is quite often absolutely nothing left, nothing at the centre. The artistic cult can be a complete sham – which is presumably why it is defended with such passion and venom, so that the person

exposing it has to be laughed out of court, jeered at as a simpleton. But when, as occasionally happens, the mask falls, the victim has a complete breakdown, and a drastic re-making of the life and personality is called for. It is of course something of a mystery that so much of artistic life attracts false personalities more than it does genuine ones, but so it is, and one should enter the artistic realms with no illusions these days. In these times the problem is exacerbated by a rampant capitalism, which visual artists who pose as "prophets" of our condition are only too willing to exploit for their own gain. There is very little joy or community or shared spirit there for the true artist, but what little there is should be treasured and nourished, in the hope of better days to come.'

Adapted and enlarged extract from an interview and article in *Suffolk Journal*, January 1997.

Abberton Reservoir

A Winter Harvest

I am a servant in Summer's Kingdom
I keep mum, and bow and scrape all day
Eat gratefully whatever scraps are given.
It is no imposition. Whether waking
Or sleeping, I lie happy on a level with the clay
And have nothing whatever to think or to say.

But the first frosts waken reflection, and the chill
Strikes a summoning bell, and I sit up sharp
Sensing my old retainers are with me still
— Mist, and the smell of woodsmoke, and a faint
Rain in the air. I make then my claim to the throne
Of Samhain. I am crowned, begin to intone

And at last to sing, drinking from the chilled wine
That is put out for me. I walk later around
December's fields, and love to find oblivion
In the big trees, whose memory has gone
Beneath the deepest root and the hardest rock in the ground.
There is a mist-gap there, a break in the line

Of being, and beneath that the great caverns
That are my kingdom. Here, where the booming sound
Is made, of bardic verse, where the blood-life is denied
And everything translated into nothingness
— Here is the workshop of all shape, all blood, all livingness.
Here is a sky beyond the sky, and ice-blue dome

Full of the black messengers of death, of the end
Of the seeing eye, of the hearing ear, of confined mind.
Here, when all shape and matter's been refined
I put away my hammer and my fire, ascend
Into the upper world, where land still wears the veil
Of a life-illusion, where the trees are still asleep

But I can read the dreams that are on their faces
Now that the solstice is long past. There is a pale
Look of a living bought by death in the March air
And everywhere suggestions and the traces
Of that nought before all being, that the world reaps
From the chanted harvest in the hidden deeps.

Poplar Grove, December, Near Copford

Cezanne's Mountain

Too easy to transform it into abstract shapes
– Those that inhabit forecourts of the mind.
If he did that, the quiddity escapes
That dour and loved resistance that we find
In obstinate things. A valid transformation
Takes more time, long staring, love, more bathing
In the air that holds us all, and long devotion
To their season day and hour. This, and the breathing
In of literal space into his spaciousness
The mental correlate of power out there.
This, and the light breathed in, the consciousness
That links us with the sun. Then he can dare
To shatter all the rocks, to pass them through
The mind's own fire that melts, makes all things new.

Waiting

The wind is cheating me of words again
Dragging its bow across the great bass strings
Of the house, wailing its vast wordless choruses.
I cannot set my mind to conscious things.
Must sit and listen, walk about my room
Suspend all thought, prohibit every sound
That might distract from this, this epic work
– Than all that's thought or written more profound.
I hear its 'Ah' of infinite loneliness
But listen harder, for an undertone
Or some dark note that's not a tone at all
That from its voiceless voice I will be shown
That all our pain is only for a season –
For this I'm dumb all day, against all sense, all reason.

Derbyshire Landscape

March Sunset, West Mersea

What kind of work is this the ending of ?
Is Tristan dying? and does Isolde sing
Of the bonfire of her hopes – and of her love
For the transformations that a death can bring?
Sweet-scented fires embrace the sky in flames
From the place of the consummation of a dream
Greater than theirs – yes, fiercer than those names
Of night they longed for, died for, in their mingled stream.
The heartbreak of the end has set us free
And brings a scent of childhood back again
And the lost freedom of the wayout sea
And fellowship of angels, fishes, men.
O sharp sea-savours, bird-cries, near and far
These are our hearth and home, and distant star.

Last Bus Home

Along the lanes this old bus, like a mole,
Is nearly blind. We love these nights, that will not be
Abolished or replaced by searching lights.
These merely, like a moon, shine on the folds,
The surface smiles of an elusive darkness.
The source lies still in shadow. And when the noon
Would make that clear at last, that face has gone –
A dream the day denies all knowledge of.
The cats' eyes guide us here, but chiefly they
Are guarding the domains of sleep. Even
The village street-lamps seem half-overcome
By airs from the kingdom they protect us from.
The lights have brought us home, but home is now
Oblivion that night's sentries brood upon.

Packing Shed, West Mersea

On a Sunset by Edward Hopper

A whole day hoping from the summer heat
A way of bringing heart into the core –
Of light, of land, of sea, of beach, of sky.
That enterprise has failed now, and no more
Is coming from that source. The coldest sunset
Leaches from the day all fire, all hope
Casting the one green hill into black shade.
Now every form retracts, for none can cope
With sunset's overwhelming cold event.
A sharp disjunction of the large and small
Drives each thin smallness to its separate cell
Too crushed to leave a sound-trace of its fall.
The human watcher's back in his cold Keep –
That place where we can neither wake nor sleep.

Kingfisher

A dead straight bolt
shot down a shaft in the air.

Flat on my feet it caught me,
an intimation of another world.

A blue flash, then
nothing.

The secret is to learn the path of flight.
To wait.

To watch a shadow
put on flesh.

August at Thorpeness

War Cemetery, Flanders

Strange our wonder is, our tilted disbelief
As we peer and pity at the plain white stones
And tell ourselves the story of the brief
Lives noted here, the multitudinous bones
— Youth's sprawling hopes made neat and null and clean
And, as in life, compelled to hold a pose
Till orders come, upon a perfect green.
We seem to make a gulf with blood-red rose
And peer across to what we must not find
— Their own and lovely and far-off repose.
Preferring that old pathos in our mind
Where pity has no end, and we can choose
To stay forever on this shore, and need not stride
To the hopeful fearful tearless farther side.

Sea-Change

Like worn-down stumps of oldest mountain ranges
These sculptures from the sea.
The smoothing hand that rubs sharp edges round
Has taken all the spite from broken glass
Removed the fangs, the bite
From rough old planks and timbers.
And everything that had a glare
A gloss to it, is now made matt.

We wonder what salubrious sea-changes
Could calm us so
Could lead us to give thanks
For losing all our edge.
On what far beaches a wise wave will toss us then
When we are bleached like tow
And all our colours are re-made
Of salt and wind and light.

Barley Fields, Near Saxmundham

The Country Soldier Returns on Leave

On a still day in summer he came back,
the lanes hot and silent.

He crept up openly upon the house
at barefaced noon
when subterfuge is least expected.

And so he caught the place
redhanded in its innocence and peace,
its stone feet bathing in the sun,
its eyes half-shuttered like a basking cat,
its brick walls purring out the heat in waves.

He sensed the inside of the house,
cool and half-darkened like a church,
and smelt the sweet dry cinnamon
swung from the censers of the kitchen stove.

He ambled round the back
to catch the garden out.

And took it in,
its hot dry scents
its powdery path
(taking the shine from his too polished toe),
the shed, and round the shed
the nettles' surreptitious life -
before he crossed the threshold of his door,
and took,
as well as taking in,
the temple-priestess of his laughing wife.

Barns Near Assington

Butterfly in March Sunshine

The east wind shakes us through,
when only a suggestion on the air.
Today the south wind blows, but I
am trembling still, uncertain
how to fly,
incapable of settling anywhere.

Now, on this stone awhile,
I close myself, and show
my dun side only;
not to disturb the frail life that is there,
nor to oppose the paleness
of the new spring air.

I would not flaunt these vivid heartfelt wings
even among the broken stems, dank grass,
and other seeming-lifeless winter things:
unless I could be sure
my new blood brings

A real life lacking here.
It's lucky I am light,
and, whether short or long, my
visitation makes no difference;
and will not tilt the beam of living thing
or barely cast a shadow on the site.

It's for myself I fly all ways
touching on everything in turn.
Tasting by this a shadow of that name
no breath must utter while it trembles there,
like wagtail balancing.
My skill is to unlearn

My vaunted colours: to fly and pale away,
to pale beyond the paleness
of the ghostly air.
To tremble and pass through
the gray and murmuring veil
of this March day.

To where that bush is burning, scarlet saffron jet
maroon vermilion purple, yellow and blue, orange and violet.

White Wind of March

The Good Meeting

I arrive, remote and polar and reduced in being
And as I knock upon the dark and winter door, I know
I have done this thing before – this willed yet
    subconscious act
Of self-annulment. Done in the anticipation of
The same act in the other man, someone I am meeting
And always for the first extended time.

And look, I was not wrong, he opens and lets me in
And yes, he has the same far-off air as myself, yet warm
Most warm, and most deeply resilient and attentive
Within a self-created emptiness. We exchange voids
And we go inside, pass to his fire-lit room, with one lamp
Standing, darkly shaded, casting a soft chastened tender light
Over his chair, while the flames' light leaps out into the gloom
And does all of the talking. For we begin in silence
Gazing, for a longish time, at the ebullient flames
And taking in the being that the dourest things regain
When we are in that Nothing before time and the world began

– Such weight and thingness in the blacksmith tongs
And in the hearth-stone such a solid base, that all the world's
Pains and wrongs seem, for the moment, gone – as though at
    the first
Forging-place of all creation. The cat, upright and staring
Into just that – ignoring all the chit-chat of the flames–
Finding that dream-state there, totality, and ideal form
And knowing her intent and steady gaze
The equal of the blaze at the hidden core.

What does it matter who begins to talk, or about what?
From such ease of being, any broached silence or subject
Will drop easeful and right words, and pass seamlessly into
Another thing, and then another thing. The words so phrased
And rhythmed, we will deem it from beyond us, not our doing.
And so it was. After a few exchanges I allow
My friend to talk, expand, and pause, and drift from theme to
    theme
– Myself both listening, darkly, deeply, easily, while still

Meersbrook Park Trees

Enjoying, as in the freedom of some dream, a tendency
To roam all over the flickering room with my glances—
From where one mad blue flame dances upon the hearth, to
    the dark
Corners, with their frolic of shadows and the fire's reflections.

We are ourselves part of that greater darkness that enfolds
All flame, and holds all urgency, all movement, in its palm.
We rest back in shadows, invisible presiding presences.
We feast on this balm of grace, which lets the fire of words be lit
Inside us, a hot star which pours out its life and being.
— While all the time we view even this as from afar
From hoarded guarded darkness, nothingness.

Our talk is both voluble and tentative, it is the freedom
Of testing on the air, and on the other, and on ourselves
Each thing that finds itself upon the tongue. We do not reify
Or over-dignify our wordings, and neither
Will we hold ourselves, nor be close-held, to anything we say.
We merely nod, both outwardly and inwardly, to those
Felicities of thought and phrase we never will remember
Not even the next day, in the prosy necessary morning.

And gradually the being that we let into our nothingness
Comes down into the business and brass tacks for which we met.
My friend moves on from chair to music shelf, and pulls down
    songs
Whose world our talk has wandered on the borders of, and
    opened up
Some fresh refinement in. He plays them, sings to them,
    while I,
Listening and drinking in, recall some poems that both
    answer to
And add, making a concert programme for a winter night.
Music and poems flourish in the void we've made for them
And quite soon we are done, and warm our hands around a cup
And at the fire again. And then we talk some more
About our own relation to the hopes beliefs imaginings
That all our 'Night Thoughts' pieces have been hinting at.

We wonder why we make this act so rare, this opening out.
Why does it take so long, before a person speaks so to a
    friend?
Our audience will be moved by what we plan
By all these things that are not spoken of.

Why is it more accepted in the code of song
To talk about the soul? Is it the fear
That all our words go wrong, betray ourselves and others, and
    estrange?
A weary knowledge of the subtle mind
That nothing ever can be rendered straight and plain? And so

Not worth the effort or the strain?
Or else we fear the pressure of our needs, or dread impinging
On another's fears, or on our own? Whatever is the reason, we
    are dumb
And speak to each other better from afar, from peopled
Solitudes. Or tell our souls to strangers on a train.

I leave at last, begin my long walk home in the frozen night.
Warmed by the fire, the cup, the music, the rare fellowship
I find a song inside me welling up, a deep dark cello note
Pitching itself halfway between the notes of old and trusted
    friends
– The earth beneath the hard frost on the paths
The polar stars.

Summer Morning

Until a man speaks
all this sound is silence.

Out in the mist, the cattle
lift their heads back and implore
the gods and graces
to continue blessing.
Man is at wonder still,
the door of his day
half-open.
Marvels in hearing how
the silence is both raucous
and unbroken.

Listens till
their utmost breath is fetched
out of the breast,
and goes on its long journey to the sun.

Longs, and is at rest.

He hears it
as a prayer of his own
reverberating round
the frontiers of the known
and the unknown.
He lets these hoarse tones shout
the hugeness he breathes in
but can't speak out.

He breathes until his breast
is full of light.

Rises.
Descends.
Still smiling at the gifts
of night
of dream
of chance.

Switches on sound
and time
and circumstance.

Wheatfields Near Peasenhall

Converted Barn

The grey wind blowing for days
Between fits of rain
The leaves dog-eared and fading
Moorland a dull stain
In the mind that watches it
Half-focused there, and half-invading
Other spheres
Through the slit of the barn-pane.

I could exist for years
Without my eyes straining to find
A vivid note.
On the same surface I am as
Dull and dun and plain
As much without the sun
As the sky, whose thoughts float
Pale, slow, seemingly in pain.

I rose this morning late
And have done nothing except
Move from bed to table, back, and back again

In baggiest old clothes, unwashed, unshaven.
I hardly care who sees me in this state
Where I, in pleasant labour, try and try
To trace out and locate
The source of a new freedom.

For here is the great good place
The big space of the barn
That, like a bell, is resonant
With inner space, vast and expanding.
Out of the window I see land and sky
Taken within that growing large embrace.
Peace without tone or flavour I enjoy
A dullness shining with a special grace.

I don't remember when the seed was sown.
It was so tiny, lay in earth so long
Season upon season. After so much
Labour without growth, it was forgotten.
Now it grows without apparent labour.
Becomes an echoing chamber where deep song
Moves free and fitfully from sound to long
And moody echoing rain-filled silence.

Hardings Boatyard, Wivenhoe II

October Days

The bonfire sun, burning down slowly
Through October's days – the sweet smoke
Of its beams pervasive, and the smell
From early morning on, through every hour
Searching our memory. These odours swell
And swell, making a space to house themselves.

How still these halls are, this great place
Of dreams and recollection. And how void
They are, even while earth's barns are full.
And all the leaves that fall here fill and fill
The vessels of the silence
With more silence still.

Echoes and shadows take possession where
The nature of true substance is not known.
Yet echoes hold their breath back for a while
And shadows in the shadows wait and wait
As in the sweet distemper of the sun
Substance and shadow still equivocate.

A robin in that silence flings
A song – a question, ending in
An upturned note. Long silence follows.
Then he looks at us. What can we say
That's pertinent, that will not break
The limpid surface of a flawless day?

Through shades and ashes to its point of rest
Low-burning sun is making its slow way.
No one need shield his face
From that mild fire.
But it is honoured with a silent tread
And on our lips our fingers are still prest.

East Mersea Beach, Late October

At the Blake Exhibition, Tate Gallery 2000

'I wander through each chartered street
Down where the chartered Thames doth flow
And see in every face I meet
Marks of weakness, marks of woe.'   *William Blake*

In those especially whose glass feet

And gaze of infinite self-love

Convey them noiselessly from street

To the revolving doors above.

A feline creature thinks it goes

Unique and brave through all the land

– The only spirit on its toes.

I've counted fifty while I stand

On these wide steps, that overview

The silent flowing smiling Thames

The great broad river that Blake knew

And one that still revolves his themes

And takes them out to that wide sea

Where calm and storm will still contend

Within the soul, for mastery.

So, while I wait here for my friend

These London bed-sit Blakes come through

And round the Blake-stall make a throng

– Self-serving notions of the True

Seems honoured there in paint and song.

For the Tate brochure is to that end

– Sedate-rebellious, wild-secure –

A crowd of attitudes that blend

The holy with the secular.

Heaven and hell are married in

A self-sufficiency of mind

A whole-in-one that cannot sin

And leaves conspicuously behind

All consolation for our death

All fellowship beyond death's door

Fibres of love and living breath

– 'We do not need these any more'.

The crowd goes in, the crowd comes out

The crowd-mind mills upon these stairs

And before Blake's ghost has time to shout

Has gone, with all its languished airs.

London Bridges

Van Gogh in Provence

The earth imprinted knowledge on the man
All summer long.
From early morning humping of the easel
To the clearing vision in the fading light
He was as pressed with every sound and smell
With every sight
As any peasant on whom labour lay
All the long day.

He came to know the morning's paths so well
Their trodden scents.
And noted with delight the bright-eyed weasel
That followed him so far along his track
Through tunnels in the wriggling dry-stone wall.
One thing at least
That did not mind his pack, and found him kind
Not some wild beast.

He shared the peasants' dawns, and shared their fields
For a whole season.
He worked through every hour as hard as they

To press the passion that was pressed on him
Into this other form. A curious way
To spend a life
They thought – who could not reason out his motive force
Nor spot his wife.

He came to know the spacings of their day
And followed them
The breakfast hour, the hot-noon rests, the grateful shades
The spring of water for the throbbing head
A late-day meal for which a cloth was spread.
And then a coolness
And the homeward tread, face glowing in the dusk
Like fire-baked clay.

They found him raging sometimes as he threw
A work away
Or stamped on it, or hung it in some tree.
This wildness lost him some of the slow trust
His patient constancy was building up.
He know that
But he raged on just the same, in sheer frustration
Flailing in the dust.

South Essex Landscape

Then, as the season burned towards its end
His rhythm came.
The sun the earth the air came charging through
Hands with the energy of mountain-streams
– Rough rugged swift unfailing and, in spate,
Unerring as the goat
That leaps from edge to edge of precipice
And does not hesitate.

He would complete three paintings in one day
His being so aflame
A nimbus round him, glowing like an angel
Or like some demon from a fiery place –
They stopped their work a little while to watch.
And saw the tears
Of sure vocation's joy, of gratitude and pain
Pour down his face.

A dim respect was growing for this friendless man.
Some sat for him –
In patience, pity, and a glimmering dawn
Of understanding what he might be at.
A peasant-woman in her floral smock

Smiled gently as she sat
Knew him a child for whom she could unlock
A portion of her warmth.

After harvest Vincent lingers on, regains
Some knowledge and some peace.
Knowledge of how we've leant on other men
And they on us, and found some solid there.
Peace that the earth has done its job once more
– And peace then finds
A secret passage to the soul's domains
And there unwinds.

Then there's October's wine-press for our pains.
And then – a nerve released – the winter rains.

Heather at Dunwich II

Two Blue Mornings in March

Who is this harsh brusque person hurrying through
The fields and barns and woods like some bleak gale?
Unconscious of the order knocked askew
And softer lights and forces that must fail
Through such assault – which still must take the blame
For the arid burnt-out ways of blustering flame.
This hard light clatters through the March-time wood
Sees only rubbish there, mere sticks and clutter
The heart-glade of the copse not understood.
For this cheap-camera eye, and fast-click shutter
Takes just the zero-instant, in the meanest focus
Strips off the nap from things – and all hocus-pocus.
Gets to the desert-heart, where nonsense ends
And thinks itself and Spring the best of friends.

Heaven has come to earth as we breathe this air!
Calm, comfortable woman with soft eyes
How did you make this be? – And with what flair
The all-round mist, from which these virtues rise
Of warmth, and purest blue of all blue skies?
You have a courtesy that you extend
To every voice and view. And, by this patience, blend
All things. Nearness and distance you can equalise.
The smallest sounds from far-off farms arrive
And scents from leaf-buds of the balsam-tree.
And in a freedom and a clarity
Rare as your generosity, all beings thrive.
And over all, this blueness you suspend
That's made of every blue, from end to end.

Old Oyster Sheds, West Mersea

Along Fenland Roads

Thoughts can be worked right through while walking.

There's
no need to be seated
housed
still and alone.

The flatness keeps us calm
the straight road keeps
the mind
one-pointed.

It does not take us long
getting
the secret
of such openness.

It takes our life, and more,
to find
it is
unending.

It is a way
into
the notion
of eternity.

Our most literal view
does not,
at last,
betray us.

Our house receives us
like
all-healing
sleep.

Puts hands
around
our thought-possessions.
Eases our dispossessions.

Wormingford Airfield, Essex

Counting the Leaves

To live in the spate of the summer
Loses us count of the leaves.
How strange it is now to remember
That place where the mind receives
Each tiniest portion of leaf
That the spring can twist out of December.

The June wind lifts the lawn sleeves
Of the birches, lifts and replaces
Lifts and replaces. We drift
And we smile. But do we recall
That difficult place behind time
Before we had faces?

Faces are first our true centre
Until we betray them.
Fused with the life of the leaves
In summer we lose them.
Better the bare homeless place
The nowhere of winter.

In the spare aspen grove of the autumn
We find that our loss
Is in learning to number again
Those few leaves remaining.
And their aerial dance on the tree
Mocks at our slow-footed wisdom.

In winter we learn not to strain
After life, for life cannot help us.
For the place of the centre is death
And we ask it to save us.
Lost between time and a god
In the held breath of midnight.

The nights hold the days in a vice
And the frost holds them both there
Sealing the ends of the earth
From decay, from fruition.
Out of creation, and back,
We follow a stiff voice

Cumberland Path

Washed at the coldest of springs
We know we can trust it.
We burrow through grains of the earth
Cleaning each one to reclaim it.
The lips of the mind are refreshed
And the cold in us sings now

And the depth and the death in us sings
In the spring, when the aspen
Is laughing all over.
And of infinite leaves none is lost
For each has its face and its motion
Distinct, and each is awake and aware

In the trembling and bright living air.
And each is a spark and a notion
In us, and each is a voice
And a light, and each is a dance.
And though we are never encumbered
The leaves are all numbered.

Haymaking

Midwinter needs these perfect summer days —
Not just to compensate the dank, the dark
But more to make connection with those ways
In which both seasons meet, and leave their mark.
Taking the winter in its finest sense
As time of dissolution and repose
Its very depth evokes June's active tense
Perfection of the form of the wild rose.
The shortest day loves its strict opposite
The day the grass dried out as crisp as thought
When all that widest arms could hold of it
Was fragrance only, weighing less than nought.
Nothings converge when June, in perfect kind,
Makes food for Winter's form-negating mind.

Potatoes at Boyton, Suffolk

Salcott Cattle Marshes

A herd of thoughts
Crosses the sky slowly.
Their mood and their demeanour
Are taken from below
From the long stretches
Without feature curve or glamour.

These salty bitten marshes
Where so few men go
Where the slow passage of cattle
Takes a long summer's day
For the traverse and the returning
—Here can a mind first settle
Then move on, unlearning
One by one, the soft illusions.
Here come strange airs and clearnesses
Strayed from another world.
No warmth in the judgments made
But the mind takes them, is saned
And fortified, sensing a hope

That must not yet be spoken
Beyond that fine blue line
Of the far horizon
Where the rigour ends, where the dooms are broken.

Salcott Marshes

From a High Tor

The climb was pleasant and easy, but the height gained is
    enough
To find world upon world around us, each circle encircling
    the last
Till, at the blue girdling horizon, the whole chord of recession
    has been sounded.

We are the kings of this castle. Do we not also manoeuvre
The spotlights that make lit islands in the fluent ocean of
    shadows?
Certainly it is our pleasure to drive dramatically apart
Things we have gained the power here to gather together
In the sublime mind made out of spaciousness
Out of the seven great strides we have made to the blue limit
    and back.

And with this huge span and force that is inside us
We seem to be partly makers of these worlds, to the blue limit
    and beyond
– The violet and out of mind.

For the vast lands bring their tribute from all sides
To us, their priest-king and centre and divine lord.
For it is us who every morning mark out the four directions
Who stride from the centre to the cardinal points and back
Allowing the world to flow into the marked veins.

And every morning Time is granted its limited permission
– To run for the one day only, to be called in at darkness.
And even in daytime, in this great primal creation
Before its fall into limited perspectives
It seems that Time as we've known it has gone from our
    minds.

In a great spaciousness there is a Time-staying, a stasis
With so much in being at once, so much coming directly
Into the arms, into the capacious barns, of the receiver-and-
    blesser.
Time as destruction has gone, and we are still eager and
    bright and sane.
For on this height we have gained real knowledge of Time
As a late sickness of creation. Time was not needed.

Time as a vanishing was a second-best, when we had grossly
    seceded.
It was imposed, when the great spatial world was betrayed
And hurtling towards a general devastation.

A large multitude in a staying spatial relation
And held in the soul of each one, in extended duration
– That should have been enough.
The growing of mutual awarenesses, without Time as oblivion
Without the losing of one thing by another's supervening.
Time is a violent and half-mad forgetting of everything
In order to have one thing clear for the split instant
That consciousness can hold it.

It is a lie that we need such Time for our life, our interest
For the provision of impulse choice and transformation.
All of that need is met in the staying spatial relation
In the mutual affectings that happen without the destruction
Of that which has undergone multiple changings.

All this we know on this height, we know that our minds
Would keep gladly forever this wealth of good things
    existing together.
We do not hunger for Time
For the occlusion of one act of awareness
For the sake of another.
We hunger precisely for what is enjoyment here
These vistas, these openings-out, unfoldings
These great and vibrant vivid gatherings
These gifts from all parts of our past in the same moment.

It is with great sadness that we go down at last
Into the narrow valleys with no view
Into the doom of Time's small blinkered eye
Into the curse of the price we must keep on paying
The pain of perpetual losing, and little knowing
Till the day we die.

Holiday Farmhouse, Lake District

In cloud and wind and rain
and in an almost darkness
for who knows how many days

This house moaned on and on
an old cracked song
of the parting of all ways

And of that final way
of watery ruin
where all are one again

In cloud and wind and rain
besieging the ancient house
the faceless dead

Who can do little more
than blunder against a door
rattle a pane

Whose tread no longer falls
upon the stairs
who have forgotten

Floors and corridors
and sudden turns
and all things lying inside the walls.

The dead walk on the water's stairway only
their feet rising and rising
floating the hands of the hours

And the numbers of the hours
away,
and us, and every stain of our lives

Down to our stone-carved names
out of the sight of the day
for ever and ever.

And the cloud and the wind and the rain
dissolve even their dead.
And all is that nothing again

Before ever
a thought fingered a brain
or a word was said.

Liddington Hill, Wiltshire

Settlers and Travellers

Our paths and stiles, and places where we stop
Whether on hill-tops, or at confluence of ways,
Where streams are forded, or where rivers bend,
At certain spots on verges of drove-roads,
Or at those spaces marked by post or stone
With room around for animals to graze
For men to stretch and lounge, and to take stock –

All these acquire a virtue by their wear and use.

And even those old places of exchange
The market-cross, the square, the portico
Where men and goods and money congregate,
Have left their savour on the hidden air.

A curious freshness springs from wear and tread
– Like that of the herb robert and the fern
That shoot from crevices in bridges there –
Those larger river bridges, those that led the step
To the small drama of the market town.

Across it waggons ground all day into the square
And the pack ponies trod their careful way

And rough men with their droves came slouching in
Grateful at last to be among their kind –
And showing this with shout and cheerful curse
And more thwacks than were needful on the rears
Of tolerant beasts. – And during all this trade
That tiniest herb was drinking from the air
And kept, clear-eyed, its dream-sharp form precise
Nourished by droplets from the ceaseless stream.

That is the sign for those good things that rise
When humans in their trades, keep their own scale,
Deal fairly, make their mark upon the land
Within the measure of that friendliness.
Then angels blend their presences with human acts
And then, the more we tread, the more the life upsprings.

But men keep green by spaces in between
Encounters – Spaces in time along that very
Track that we wear down – but, more than these –
Those spaces of the air, of space itself, of light,
Those larger presences, those shouting wrestling angels

There, in the interpenetration of sun's rays
With veils of cloud, of rain, sweeping in droves across
And taking the moorlands up to galloping skies.

Yorkshire Plain

For in that swirl, and fusing elements,
Shaking the feeling mind from rigid shapes –
Men find they can be murmured to of loss.
For death and losses past can be contained
And loss and death to come envisaged there
In copious space and air. And in that drama
Of the striding light, its partial triumphs,
Rests, and dark occlusions, victories won
Late in the lowering day, when sudden
Sun breaks clear, and with vast passion all
That's green transfuses – then an unconscious
Consolation seals men's hearts. The mind itself,
Feeling that transparency of green
Sensing it both receive and give out the sun's rays
Like emerald jewels, and in unknowing rapture
Lifted up, looks down to earth again.
And is content to set that gritty rock
That black opaque impenetrable night
Against the radiance. Rejoices in
A roughness in this world, determines to enjoy it
Juxtaposed to thoroughgoing penetrating
Shattering light. 'Thus will my soul stay green'
– His hidden cry – 'Green, by remaining rough and black!

My house, my hearth, my bed, my wife, my child.
Thus my companions and my travelling life.'

He hurries on now, as the dark comes down
Past all those places that are passages
And nothing else – not to be stopped at, looked at,
Even thought about. For they reject
Man's searching glance, man's soul – give nothing back.

First passing by some hamlet in the dusk
And the arriving at the upland town,
He carries space inside him, and receives
The nods of streets, the smile of market-cross.
Worn flagstones welcome him, and bring him peace.
He stops, and feels the spire salute him from its place.
The houses are like arms, the faces at
The windows are like gods and angels.
And that soft light, the light inside an inn,

Naming itself against the siege of demons
And of darkness – that, at this latening hour
Is heaven's light.

August Evening, Saxmundham

Allotment in April

Birdsong all day, vehement, strong
Tough sailors
In the rigging of the hedges
Shouting, loud and long –
Big-chested sounds
Out of the tiniest bills –
Strong trills that stir
The solid air
Sharp notes spiking
And digging there
To let sound in
And spread it round.
The skylarks are shaking
Earth from their hair
Flicking the spires
Of rooting twitch
Onto the pyres for burning
– Their anger and impatience
Gives them an energy
That never tires.

At pink dusk
Only the blackbird sings.
His song stabs at
Our deepest memories
Of old earth-things –
Unpicks
The longest-rusted wires
And hardened strings.

Hardings Boatyard, Wivenhoe I

October Angel

Late Summer was a sprawling oaf, and said
'Lie down near me, and make an easy bed
Under a thatch of leaves or space of sky.
And doze and dream and sleep, and do not fear
The drift of stars, or turning of the year.
I am a friendly god, and how would I
Let anything outrun or pass you by?'

But who, then, is this angel with the piercing eye
Impatient look, and one that does not smile
Who drives a cloud-pack fast, and mile on mile
Across this blue, this Eden in the sky –
This gate that opens once, and not for long
And by that briefness, breaks hearts into song?

The dry leaves scratch the ground, with an enormous sound.

November Night at Bamford Community

No stain of light or colour
in the country night.
I take with me to bed
a draught of darkness, black
and intense
Lie listening on my back
and ceding precedence to
the wordless wind

The mind driven and scattered like the leaves out there
or like the naked bushes, whistled through

Only unfettered nothings of black driving air
alert what's left of me
and bring it closer to
that deep nowhere
hidden within the wind
that moans and labours long,
but only seems to be a lonely song.

I float down sleep's dark stream
like any child that nods off
while the tale is telling.
Trusting the end that beckons from a dream.

Heather at Dunwich I

A Vision

I moved across to rake the fire
   and as I fumbled there
A vision leapt up like a flame
   lifted my every hair.

I saw the moment of my birth
   and moment of my death
With no more time between them
   than between breath and breath.

Like a sudden wind that catches up
   one leaf upon a tree
This terror seized me, whirled me round
   and made my wide eyes see

Such horrors as we find in sleep
   forcing the voiceless scream
Till the whirlwind stopped, I lived again
   our usual timeless dream.

For Time was the thing the vision showed
   a course where lightnings run.
Is it in mercy to us all
   he hides his shattering sun?

I know a dangerous child in me
   that dares beyond his age.
It hurries on and harries Time
   to show his strongest rage.

And Time has shaken out a seed
   that roots itself and grows
Into a tree that trembles when
   the softest south wind blows.

From the Sussex Downs

Widower

Crosses the park slowly
Drinks from the wine
Of the dusk of November

Those children's cries
Their figures as they flit
In and out of the shades

The smell of the gardens'
Stifled fires
– Strong, and as though fresh

As though the stars' lamps
From their lavishness
Were lately struck and lit.

Stars, in the damp air
Burn faintly
Unestablished there.

As the dark presses
And closes
A ghost-form slips from the man

And goes forward
– To make, in the dark house
A fire like roses.

Wapping Pier

A Winter Meditation

Bliss of the fire-drowse, following those walking hours in wind
  and light.
Let darkness fill the room, and watch the flames that dark
  and the night enclose
Push out their buds and leaves, and flourish like a rose.
And in the after-images, which inner sight
Enjoys in the quietness – the earth, the woods, the bright
Clouds skimming across repeated skies – detachment grows.
Mind pulls from its moorings in our time and space, tires
Of the gravity imposed, monotonies of up and down, of near
  and far
Of fadings and of vanishings – wherever mind inquires –
Of memories buried deep, beyond the furthest star.

Tree-roots grow down from heaven, the sun goes
  underground.
Mind at the centre of its new-found space, learns freely to dispose
The stars and stones, the clouds and streams and seas. Freely
  they round
And shift their place, spinning like firewheels, seeking their
  repose

Only when active will commands. The wind-sweep of time is
  stilled.
The wand that signs rest or motion, is in the hand of power
That seizes many things at once, and slows the hour.
– But first it was from looking all day long that mind was
  filled
With this unfailing energy. The jolt of colours lit this sudden
  fire
That subjugates the worlds, burns without ceasing, stays
  entire.

Winter Scene Near Easthorpe

The Churchyard

We keep a certain loyalty to graves.
In curious ways, to those of perfect strangers.
Arriving at the solitary church, a mile
or more from any place, the lands around
composing into pious hands
in some good lady's lap.

The slightest wind among the branches
stirs
some memory of those we've never known.
Or starts a tender feeling
for we know not what.
Is it our own envisaged burial plot
visited by strangers and the wind
or by some lover of high dream ?
Or is it being buried with our loves
and feeling gratitude for strangers' homage there?

These tombs are for the living, not the dead.
They house our sighs for transient conjunctions.
They house regrets
for quirks seen once, that never will be seen again,
reflections of ourselves in passing strangers' eyes.
In tombs we tip such lumber of our lives.
We sigh here, as we sever
our connections, one by one.
Here, among strangers, learning
to be a stranger to our lasting loves
and to ourselves.

High Bradfield Churchyard, Yorkshire

The Cat Sat on the Mat

Sometimes
upon all fours
returning the red-hot blaze
with steady gaze

And sometimes limp
and helpless, with no claws
lying upon her side
curled like a shrimp.

And sometimes sitting proud
and drawn up high.
A rock-carved Buddha-head
clear above cloud.

Her front legs then
the entrance to a temple.
A dim dark land
the simple clever monkeys
never understand.

Such are mere men
whose thoughts lack steadfastness.
Who at their highest reach
have everything to learn
and nought to teach.

So say her eyes
her whiskers and her smile,
her bliss-awareness
fixed in the zenith of all skies.

Willow Grove, Wiston

The Flowers of the Shingle

For the seven lost years of my youth
This shingle shore, its wolf-grey sea
Its sky, a tower of barren stone

These stood as background to my dark
Difficult ways – though that was strange
For I was raised inland, softly

And this hard shore I'd seen once
Only. That proved to be enough.
It became a grey foreboding

A confirming symbol of all
That I found sterile in myself –
Which was most things in those days.

My root in those richer soils
With the surround of equable air
Refused to take. I felt alone

Baffled, gasping for water
In the well-watered smiling place.
I became numb, dumb, friendless

And that image rose before me
That yellow skull of a sky
Death-dealing wolf-toothed wind-toothed sea

And the sterile shingle, low-value
Dull rejected coin, with no other use.
Yet the whole turned from threat to friend

In my desolation, a grim
Consoling, a place of strange refuge.
Here there was no obligation

To root or grow or flower
To be sprightly, or smile, or
Make polite conversation.

Butley River

I had no notion flowers grew there.
But as I made it my friend
Some root of me must have taken

For now, in these after- years
As I live not far from these shores
I've made these tough plants my own

That had only the sand, small stone
And the difficult dry shingle
To grow from. Sea-lupin, my friend!

Where did you find the sun's gold
And the full-freighted green of the earth?
And you, you florid yellow-horned poppy

I ask you the same question.
And then you, you pinks and whites
Of the bladder sea-campion

Where did you change dull coin
For this new dispensation?
Many things glaucous and strange

Grow on this place, as though
Half from the under-waters
— Like Wild Men of Orford that landsmen

Cannot quite place in the order
Of rational being. I know myself
One of these, know my own kin at last

And can bless them and smile these days
As they bloom in the stony ways
And amaze the fresh traveller here.

I'd make now my thing to be won
My holy aspiration, that
Young sea-holly of the soft leaves

That hard-won half-sea beauty
With the blue scabious flower
And all the spite gone.

Summer Evening at Boxted

Estuary

1

Here we are again

my old self

and all its old antagonists

meeting in summer on the bleak sea-wall,

raised above meadows

the wind defining me again

for the old encounter

as I stroll out laughing from my stagnant corner

mouthing at air

and eating eating

the wind

and all that is not myself,

tide

and the sea-wrack

and the slack mud-filled

fold

of the sea's warm edge

flaccid and fetid

and flapping limply

along the hot slabs of the little bays

a nudge a whisper

a succulent fable

rocking of dead shells of tiny crabs

as in a half-forgotten cradle

And the long grass seeds and blows in the hot
    June wind

and the hillside barley

waves and weaves

as though performing —

and my self looks on again

with the same harsh worriting and ravenous eye

wanting release

from its own obsessive staring

wanting to feel sufficiency in their sufficiency

and failing —

Still going on

beneath their surfaces

still foraging and fumbling,

scouring the land

for all the hidden talents that it holds

Low Tide, West Mersea

looking for players
to play the parts assigned
in the imagined heaven
of my never quiet mind.

2

Perhaps I can be easy all the same
not tax the land too hard
for this one day?
Shall I just lightly with these images
as though for the first fresh time
just lightly play?

I reach a point of turning
where the wall points home,
the wide sea points another way.

Feet founder and stop
as the longbow of my wishing
shoots me clean away
from land and the land's infirmities.

One seaward impulse
then my self comes back

almost to resignatioin
in this long-loved place.

But O, my life is getting late
I say aloud
and will not rest much longer
in these half-formed things.
The arrow of my wish
shoots out again
is lost
in blinding cloud.

3

O wind, and the open sea!
Shake me, before I turn for home,
with something better than your bad infinity.

O Sun, help me upon this strand

That sword of light you lay
across those distant waters
past all thought of land

Give me
Into my hand.

Seascale Beach, Cumberland

The Opening

Beneath the towering cloud the ocean shines.

The rocks' repose is bliss,
as waves slip into peaceful lapping lines
and meet the shore-line with a long-drawn kiss.

There is a sense that every place is now
feeling such life upon its stricken brow
that every wintry evil melts away,
and stretched-out dead ones to the living say
'Love!' And all the living feel
the tender proffered mouth towards them steal
of that vague spirit, spread through everything:
fevers, in shadows and in bliss extinguishing.
Recesses opening up in every part,
in limbs and breasts and eyes and scanted heart,
for the reception of the sacred sap.
A great peace from on high begins to lap around.
The grasses push through cracks in hardened ground.
The eggs hatch out. The soul is warm and sound.
The infinite seems full of trembling leaves.
Dawn's white horses neigh, the earth receives

the first steps of the wind, and hears as heretofore,
the bolt slid back upon the sonorous door.
The sparrow, with a sprite-like flickering motion
teases the smiling hugeness of the ocean.
The air plays with the fly, the eagle with the foam.
The solemn labourer furrows the dark loam,
setting the page out clearly and in line
on which the poem of harvest will soon shine.
Some fishermen, beneath a vine-branch there,
see a strange vision of the sea and air;
a dazzling dream far off in which occurred
the ocean like a hydra, and the cloud a bird.
And now, from where a mother rocks her child,
a gleam sets out, the flowers, fields and wild
waves gilding; becoming light at last
on touching on that tomb which lies close fast
beside the tower which contains the bell.
The day is penetrating blackest hell.
It searches out that shade, to kiss its brow
beneath the savage gloomy waters. Now
all is soft calm happy and assuaged, at one,
God looking on.

Translation of a poem by Victor Hugo, 'L'Eclaircie'

High Tide, Tollesbury

The Old Oak

Old oak, spreading your branches
Wide into the air
And into earth
Striking your solid roots.
Neither earth's shaking
Nor those aerial powers
That from the North
Upon the world are loosed
Not biting showers
Nor anything that Winter
On the land
Can summon or command

Nothing of these can shift you
From that place
Where you stand steadfast
And grow up with grace.

As a true image of my faith you stand
Unmoved by mere events
Dealt by whatever hand.

One plot of ground
Ever and ever you embrace.
By you it is made fruitful
And by you it is most strongly
And together bound.
Through deepest earth extend
Your roots.
To every generous soul
You are a welcome friend.

And I, that follow you
Now bend my spirit, and my sense and mind
To one firm end.

Translation of a poem by Giordano Bruno

Messing Airfield

Colne Valley Line 1956

One journey on a train recalls that dream.
Evening, late summer, and a light
that was a rose
that flowered from the earth's creative heart.
The grimy carriage let the radiance in;
rode over points, and clanked
its chains, and laughed.
It seemed I'd waited all my eighteen years
to catch this train,
cold and uncertain, in a windy place.
It was my first sigh of relief;
and then my first wholehearted smile.
The words rose up inside me, and broke out
– There's going to be a harvest !
There's going to be a harvest after all. –

How cold came back to claim me for its own,
how ripened fields went down with wilt and blight,
is something I recall,
but cannot understand at all, at all.

Harvest Song

Here, by a fallen willow
On a burning day
The leaves are thinned and yellow
And the down-seeds stray
Among the ragged thistles.

The grass is spent and over
And the willow lies prone
Where the cattle rub their muzzles.
Here, where heat-flies drone
Not one bird whistles.

But only the light mind puzzles
At the way a deep voice sings
Below the dry well's whispers
Against these dried-up things

O willow, fading willow
Now the grains lie in their store
I'll take thistles for a pillow
And for bed the hard-earth floor.

Walton Backwaters, Summer

The Sacred Space: The Poetry of David Britton

Goblet d'Alviella's *Migration of Symbols* traces the image of the sacred tree to Mesopotamia and links it with the concept of a life force, fecundity and universal regeneration. *Grimm's Teutonic Mythology* says that for the forest-dwelling Teutons, the tree was divine. The word for *temple* also meant *wood* and 'the . . . worship of the people has its seat in the grove', according to Grimm. The holly is one of the seven noble and sacred trees of the Iron Age temple grove. It rules the eighth month, August, the month of harvest. The Green Knight who challenges Sir Gawain (the Oak Knight) bears a mace of holly and finally shows mercy to the Oak Knight. In Welsh myth, the Holly Knight and the Oak Knight fight every May Day until Doomsday. Christ assumed the aspect of the Holly King in mediaeval thought and thus the holly was glorified above the oak. 'Of all the trees that are in the wood/The holly bears the crown', says the carol; the holly's properties are equated with aspects of Christ's life and so holly means holy.

It is fitting then that this poet's first collection of poems is entitled *The Grove of Hollies*, for the title reflects his sense of the sacred in nature. It is significant that the quotation he chose to illustrate holly's meaning for him is concerned not only with the sacralisation of nature but also with the joy of human creativity and popular art. Are sacred groves all dead, now that we scarcely have enough trees left to keep this planet alive? This poet finds some promise and hope within nature yet, and elsewhere, for he believes that 'the Space and Time world we live in at present, is made meaningful by reference to a larger sacred structure which subsumes them and is able to express spiritual realities through them'. At some points the light burns low, but a guttering flame is better than no flame, as he writes in the poem entitled *The Grove of Hollies*; there is a 'something' 'almost' erased in him and others who 'keep/A residue of this once potent faith', reduced to a 'half-formed thought'.

These others are close to the earth and to the crafts and traditions of the people, solitary landworkers, hedgers, ditchers, men who can accept the poet as a worker like them doing his essential work of meditating and making amongst their labours. The poet's meditation sacralises their labour as he conjures it up in his mind's eye, the lone ploughman labouring as the Angelus bell sounds, and 'the bell, the plough, the arm, the earth, the soul' are transfigured by the human beauty of man's fruitful labour on the earth and by spiritual realities also, for the plough turns over not just soil but heavenly energies. Men like these are a dying breed and will be lost in the desecrating tide of cold, rational capitalism.

It is April; no ploughman walks this field, a tractor harrows the earth. From these dark thoughts, the poet turns. Within his holly grove, a new meditation takes place. It is related to the meditations recalled in the opening stanzas of the poem, spiritual work done by monks which was rooted in a living tradition ('everyone believed it') – related, but not the same. How can a feeling belief in 'the inter-connectedness of all salvation' survive amidst the bleak emptiness of a world centred upon materialism? Under the arch and dip of the holly branches, the poet reaches a state of sublime, restful joy; knowing that man, poet, sun and spring are whole, are the centre and that the seasons still need our response. The need and the response are beautifully considered in David Britton's poetry.

'It takes a fire within to respond to the fire that is locked inside prosaic things, dull winter things', he writes elsewhere. He believes that there should not be a wide division between mystical states, poetical inspiration and the rest of human experience; furthermore, he strives in his work to offer us a share in his soul-struggle and in the deeper truths. In the short, hushed lines of *Along Fenland Roads*, we experience a moment of being, of knowledge. The poem quiets the reader, such is its meditative force. It breathes silence. Within and because of the landscape, there is a stillness and a receiving and the mind is not fragmented.

Harvest Song is not a scene of reaping and gathering. The harvest is over and stored in the granary; what remains? The Dry Tree. This was used the mediaeval writers as a symbol of the death which entered the world at the fall but which was overcome by Christ's sacrifice. According to Malory, 'by the bare tree betokenyth the worlde, which ys naked and nedy, withoute fruyte, but if hit com of oure Lorde'. These underlying meanings enrich the poem, but the image of the dry tree is wonderfully transformed by this poet. One of his great gifts is in showing us the *haecceitas* of the natural world in all its purity and here we see that the dry tree is good as it is, a homely and useful tree, on which the cattle innocently rub their muzzles. The well is dry too; nevertheless, a song arises, and so hope arises in the scorched barrenness, for sun-scorching can be part of the life rhythm and what remains, however harsh, is right in its thisness, whether thistles for a pillow or the hard earth for a bed.

Settlers and Travellers opens with a scene of pre-capitalist trading, a ceaseless stream of humanity engaging in fair association and fellowship. This goodness the poet sees as sacred – 'then Angels blend their presences with human acts' – and by joining with each other and with animals too in this age-old union, 'the more the life springs', by which the poet means all life, including even the Herb Robert and the fern which keep their shapes of perfection whether we regard them or not. These unconsidered plants live in right and perfect association with air and water and even with humanity, growing in the crevices of stone bridges. These bridges, made by man from the earth's 'skin and surface' (as another poet once put it) contain that tiny unregarded flowering of life. Community contains the sacred, certainly; the Herb Robert and the fern are part of the ecological and the sacred structures of life; this much the poet has made clear.

What keeps man's spirit alive and growing is the burden of the second half of his poem. What is growing and burning and flowering within man as he journeys through the uneventful flow of existence? For this he must look beyond flower and market-cross to the spaces in between, to light, the sky, where other angels dwell, angels not content to blend and bless but seeking rather to 'shake the feeling mind' out of its rigidity into the pain of death and loss. Out of this and out of the divine green beauty of the natural world, we are content, rejoice even, in our lot, caught between the darkness and the light, death, loss and rapture, and we return to the rough gritty rock of mundanity and community, our fellow-travellers, the lights and the inn and the fire, which make life sweet.

October Angel is a poem that makes one shiver - the hair rises on one's head as if in fear, and tears come to the eyes. There is a strong contrast between the two verses, the movement from ease and warmth to the terrifying end and challenging angel. There is a sustained movement and complete flow in the second verse, full of the urgency of the angel, and very beautiful. There is an exact and perfect mixture of both the sorrow and the fear of transience, and in 'breaks hearts into song' – hearts are broken but into something creative and expressive – there is both suffering and a redemption. Both layers of meaning are wonderfully present in that phrase.

We see, in the first verse, the attraction of not having to fear – not having to fear the movement of the universe, time, the things we can't alter and that leave us helpless. And yet there's an easy danger in the word 'doze'. Dreaming is a good thing, but not allied to a certain lazy stupidity in 'doze'. 'Oaf' warns too.

In the last line, the poet is not scared of allowing 'ground/ sound'. That line has quietness, an ominousness, a mystery.

North Yorkshire Moors

The resonances are interesting – the personifications, the capturing of the spirit of season. The poem draws easily yet not over-allusively on all that, resting on the traditions lightly and rising above them. 'Lie down near me' – could it even be that there is a temptation to dissolution and death behind this invitation? If so, the message isn't unduly heavy, for it is lightened by the mellow 'easy bed' and 'thatch of leaves'. Both verses are strings of phrases joined by 'and', and so it is amazing to realize how the first verse gives the impression of sprawling laziness and the second, such speed, and urgency. "This gate that opens once, and not for long" – is a line that stays with the reader.

A Winter Harvest

Again, the poet has both used and transformed the 'seasonal' tradition. There's a mysterious ancientness here that appeals greatly to me, and the contrast between the simplicity of the first stanza and the poem's growing complexity I like very much. I've been reading and re-reading it and noticing the idea of a sort of life-in-death – absolutely the *winterness* of winter – in the movement back and forth between oblivion/memory, blood/life/ nothingness, life-illusion/dream – to 'a living brought by death', 'that nought before all being' – gradually it becomes clearer, and the beautiful rhythmic recurrence of nature is *there* in all

its mysterious creativity and cruelty. Also, one can take an almost childish pleasure in being told this story, winter's story as he comes into his kingdom, walks among the trees and into his workshops. This poem is built up in such an effective way. If we just let the eye wander over the lines and pick out various words and phrases – 'bardic verse', 'blood-life', 'workshop', 'shape', 'my hammer and my fire', 'mist-gap', we can sense so many allusions and so much richness, all suggested, not spelt out, a beautifully *concentrated* richness.

The Good Meeting

The first six lines of the poem are delightful. They contain the whole of the poem, and their rhythm contains the meaning and the mood. They create a sort of hush, in which we wait for their extension. And this hush happens in the second verse as it 'begin[s] in silence' and creates the quality of it in the firelit interior. I like the contrast between the concrete, the 'thingness' of things, and 'nothingness' (which is repeated), between the simplicity of the intimacy ('what does it matter . . .') and the mystic quality of the 'balm of grace', the 'brass tacks' and 'the greater darkness'; and when the words 'fire' and 'cup' are repeated, their echo suggests symbolic values and they have resonance. I feel that lots of poetic attempts at description along the lines of 'we did X, then we did Y' are clumsy and fall flat. This doesn't; it shows the 'ease of being' in which one can 'speak so' to a friend, in which cup and fire are themselves in their thinginess, and the rhythm encloses the intimacy. It's perfect, then to have the series of questions following on from it. And then the poet actually makes the 'music' of the last six lines – it comes beautifully alive in the last two lines.

Linda Miller
(Linda has an Honours Degree in English from Somerville College, Oxford and has written and published articles for the William Morris Society.)

The Poetry of Postures

It is very frustrating to be kept waiting for over six months after one has sent off a batch of poems to a magazine, but I am told that six months to a year is now standard, not a sign of dilatoriness on the part of the editors. At 65, I am in the position of remembering a time when magazines responded within a month, and three months was generally regarded as the uttermost limit.

Obviously the cause of the problem is the vast number of people writing poems now, and expecting publication. This is a ridiculous situation. It is not 'in the nature of things' that there will be some 5,000 talented poets, not in a thousand years, far less within a decade! Not even in Elizabethan times could this country boast more than twenty or thirty poets whose work has stood the test of time. What we have nowadays is a culture in which everyone wants to be a creator, and hardly anyone wants to be a mere audience. Yet without an audience, the arts lose most of their point. Also, if you are a poet, the reading of 'the tradition', and of your contemporaries, has until recently been accepted as part of the apprenticeship of a writer.

When I say 'recently', I mean as recently as ten or fifteen years ago. In my own adolescence in the 1950s, those of us who were interested in poetry at all, read and welcomed, for instance, Larkin's work when it came out. We did not expect to become instant Larkins ourselves. There was a respect for craft, and for qualities that would take some time to achieve. In my twenties and thirties I continued to read (and was in no way unusual in this), both 'the tradition', and such new work as seemed worthwhile. For myself, my attitude to a poet such as R. S. Thomas, and to some of Ted Hughes's work, was one of considerable veneration. Also, I worked full-time at my own poetry for two or three years before I considered sending some out for publication. It seemed right to curb a little one's inevitable conviction of one's own instantaneous genius, and to recognise that a process of apprenticeship was the sensible norm. Of course there are important exceptions to this in the history of poetry, when people in their first youth pour out their best work, but it is still the best general rule.

Art as Self-Expression has been an element in the cultural scene for the whole of the last century, but it was only an element, and never has its influence been so widespread and so malign as it is now. The notion of acquiring a culture, of setting one's own enthusiasm and desire for expression against a background of a respected tradition of practice, has just about disappeared.

What seems to have happened is that the notion of Art as Self-Expression has been conflated with the more recent notions of Post-modernism, and also of Political Correctness. In these philosophies nothing must ever be construed as being better than anything else. Works of art are simply the expressions of different sub-groups and tendencies in Society, and enjoy a sort of natural right to be represented on the cultural platform. There is almost no such thing as either good poetry or bad poetry. Everything speaks from a legitimate 'point of view', or is 'differently abled'. All artists are equal.

This is not yet true everywhere, thank heavens, but in some quarters it is even worse than I have stated it. In those quarters some artists are indeed 'more equal than others', and this in the worst possible sense. It is precisely those with the right point of view, or posture, or those with the right disadvantage, who become the privileged ones. An insolent young man from the Arts Council comes into the office of a long-standing magazine to announce the withdrawal of its Arts Council grant.

And his reasons? ' There are too many poems by people over 25.' Also, 'there are too many by white people. Where is your quota of ethnic minorities? And where is your register of disabled poets, and why are they receiving no special support? And where are your performance artists? You are too staid and traditional, and you don't represent the currents of a multi-cultural and post-modernist society. You persist in talking about "standards", when post-modernism shows that this is an absolutist stance, and is totally unacceptable.'

This is no fantasy, this happened, and will continue to happen. Most of the poetry money from certain Arts Councils goes to support the exhibitionistic and posturing young arseholes who do 'performance poetry'.

There is no surer way of doing harm to these good causes, and to what could be called the legitimate interests of young people in general, than to go about things in this particular way. People who have any sense of the 'fitness of things' are incensed by these methods and attitudes.

As I sit here now, and feel a volcanic rage arising at these absurdities, I actually feel that I hate all young people with a bottomless hatred. Performance poets I genuinely do loathe and abominate, but in all the other cases the fear and loathing is largely a miasma created by the false presentations of reality by these afficionados of Political Correctness. *They* create the false image, and many of us are betrayed into hating a mirage.

However, 'youth culture' is an actual evil, not just a mirage, and it has certainly got worse in the last ten or fifteen years or so. I am a painter as well as a poet, and in my youth I accepted the fact that you did not receive big awards and special recognition until you had first been properly trained and had built up, over a considerable number of years, a body of good work. The Saatchi and Nicholas Serota regimes have changed all that. They have created a system by which awards and recognition go to young people on account of their youth alone. Any pretence of actual *quality* in the work is presented and is adjudged in terms of a sort of *quantity* called youthfulness, or rather, adolescence, embodying outrageousness, the desire to shock, and 'originality' (always falsely conceived). The arrogance and insolence of youth are given massive encouragement while in their full natural flow, creating the most dire abortions, both of work and personality. That unspeakable ignoramus Tracey Emin brandishes the impressive label 'Conceptual Artist' to dignify her vacuity and mendacity, while the ridiculous Sarah Lucas practises her studied 'black looks' for the cameras, and perpetuates adolescent embarrassments that, left to themselves, would have died years sooner by the natural death that is called adulthood. Meanwhile good artists who have worked for a lifetime are sidelined and ignored.

To return to the question of poetry today. What we need is a steady and large return to the culture of the reading of poetry. The writing of poetry is a very special gift, and, as Iris Murdoch often said, probably the hardest of all the arts to do really well. There are very few genuine poets in any generation, and even these will write much that will not last. Most of the poetry that is written, in any age, is rubbish, and some of the rubbish is written by good poets. Yet the assumption today seems to be that the writing of poetry is the easiest of all the arts. The basis for this attitude seems to be that since we all, as human beings, use language, then we can all, with a little effort, become poets. And, of course, we all have our 'point of view', and any and every 'point of view' is now regarded as legitimate. This is a fallacy of a very simplistic kind, and needs a strong corrective.

The culture of the reading and the valuing and the actual *treasuring* of poetry is, I believe, the most powerful element in any corrective regime. When I say we should read poetry for *illumination*, naturally some idiot will get up and say that we read it for *enjoyment*, creating thereby a polarisation between so-called 'seriousness' and so-called 'fun' that is in no way intended by the use of the term 'illumination'. But the older generations of poetry-readers will have understood my meaning. For generations of readers, who learned poems by heart, certain poems became talismans, or magic keys to unlock certain doors when these needed to be unlocked. Poems have been the accompaniment of a developing spiritual life, even for those

Landscape Near Penistone, Yorkshire

97

who did not use that notion. But any life that experiences occasional illumination, and gives value and reality to that idea, and lives its life so that that illumination will be enlarged, and uses poetry towards that end, is a spiritual life. And a life so lived makes no mistake when it credits poetry with the power to illuminate the soul. Many thousands of people have found this to be so, not only in the ordinary periods of struggle that are part of most lives, but also in times of grave crisis.

I am not talking of Patience Strong here, I am talking of *quality*, of a growing depth and subtlety of appreciation of poetry as a life itself grows more complex and assured. One of the great validations of poetry is that it is found to answer even better to our developed psyche that to the relatively undeveloped psyche of adolescence and youth in which a passion for it is usually born. We had thought perhaps to outgrow it, to regard its restorative magic as a phenomenon of adolescence itself. But we find that poetry knows us better than we know ourselves. It searches us out. It finds us again, rather than us finding it. Certain remembered lines reach into us and shake us more than of old. That is often the experience of older people. It shocks us again by its power. We are moved to tears – or, as Wordsworth said, to 'thoughts too deep for tears'. It is more than literature, it is a contact with spiritual reality. And renewed contact with its *real quality and its*

healing power convinces most people that *writing* it is beyond their powers. It is enough to appropriate it for their lives.

Why then do so many people now ignore the very real joys of a lifetime lived alongside poetry, in the reading and love of poetry, for the dubious benefits of 'becoming an artist' themselves? Firstly, I suppose, because they do not believe that the mere reading of poetry will in fact provide the satisfactions I have been outlining. And certainly it won't unless a life is lived with a certain passion and hope. Poetry is not a drug, that will do the trick no matter what we believe and how we live. Secondly, not crediting the traditional satisfactions of reading, there is instead the certain satisfaction of gratified vanity to fall back on and to cherish at all times. And thirdly, there is the powerful illusion of gratified Self-Expression, whether through the indulgence of violent language and imagery, or of 'humour' (usually the most revolting and tiresome facetiousness), or of ironic self-deprecatory tracts (very English, and absolutely ghastly), or of therapeutic lengthy confessionals (very apparently 'liberating' for repressed Englishmen), or of topicality and being cleverly up-to-date, or being surrealistically and wildly metaphysical, and so on.

But the result of all this, as I have already said, is that while there are thousands writing this rubbish, and having it published in poetry magazines, almost no one is reading it. How therefore is vanity to be gratified? And how is Self-Expression to be enjoyed if no one else is very much enjoying one's Self-Expression? It does rather blunt the edge of it, if we are honest with ourselves. One might have thought that the great army of Self-Expressers would generously give themselves to the appreciation of other Self-Expressers, but they don't, and that is the end of the matter. Increasingly, the small amount of real poetry that is still produced is hardly noticed or heard in all this clamour.

Where does this leave the Poetry Editors? I suppose those of them who are still sane after wading through thousands upon thousands of poems every few months would much prefer it if there were far fewer contributors, and a larger number of people who subscribed to the magazine in order to read and enjoy good poetry. There are others no doubt who welcome the deluge as a sign of vitality and democracy. These people are mad – but whether as a result of years of deluge, or from an initial and original madness, it is not always possible to say. But populist madness certainly exists.

Do those who would welcome fewer poets and more readers actually know what they are doing well enough to spot the good poets and provide their readers, nay, even educate their readers, with material of appropriate quality? It takes no qualifications whatsoever, except a capacity for unrelenting unpaid work, to become an editor of a Poetry Magazine, and often enough vanity and Self-Expression are motives as strong as in would-be poets. There is also the gratification of the wielding of the powers of life and death. And of course many are poets themselves as well as editors

My feeling, from looking at some fifty or sixty magazines, is that most of the Editors are pursuing false trails. It doesn't take long to discover the particular mind-set, attitudes and values of an Editor. You can all too easily tell what he or she is looking for, and where these mind-sets are obvious, it is not poetry as such that is being sought, but attitudes, and indeed postures, that chime with those of the editor. Typical postures are those connected with social relevance or topicality; or being sexually shocking, or fashionably violent; or being a hard political commentator, without heart or soul; or enjoying an academic and serious and critical and 'intelligent' stance. This last could be called The Academy of Critical Intelligence and Comprehensive Nullity. There is a posture of nihilism; there is a posture of tapping the unconscious, and a posture of becoming a wild maenad. There are many more, and a complete phenomenology of current postures would be interesting (for another occasion?). But the general rule seems to be that if the piece of writing expresses the desired posture intelligibly, it is poetry, and should be published

Taking up a 'posture' may also be a more or less unconscious way of dealing with the huge bulk of poems submitted, a method of 'breaking up bulk'. If so, it is a damnably bad way. It breaks the bulk, but it does not find the poetry.

There *is* something called poetry, and it is only this that should be looked for, not some set of special attitudes. If one knows the experience of real poetry it doesn't actually take long to spot if a piece of writing has a chance of being poetry or not. It is either established in the first six to eight lines, or it is not going to be established at all. The quality is undefinable, but has to do with a mysterious and compelling rhythm appropriate to the subject matter. This marriage of rhythm and content is the product of inspiration, and there is no substitute for it. Craftmanship can only refine and polish, not create it, and the same goes for all the 'rules', the 'do's and don'ts, of writing poetry. If you don't know this rhythm, and can't spot it, or its absence, you shouldn't be editing a poetry magazine. Knowing it, really knowing it, 'breaks up bulk' more surely and quickly and creatively than anything else. But this has to be done from the outset, otherwise the bulk will instead break

the editor, dissolve the judgment in an ocean of nonsense, and drive him or her mad beyond recovery. This, I fear, is happening far and wide.

Norfolk Fields and Dunes

The Paintings of Stanley Royle: A Personal Reaction from an East Anglian Landscapist

(from the Sheffield Art Review 1992 – Editor: Eric Mackerness)

When I first came to live in Sheffield in 1985 I had been painting the East Anglian scene for over ten years, and had lived in Essex and Suffolk for most of the previous twenty-five. In my very early efforts with the brush, before I began to work seriously, I used to find the Essex landscape flat and boring, and I used to invent background hills where I could. I had not learnt to peer through to the long distances; I had not yet learnt to be fascinated by the thin pencil lines of far fields and the tiny suggestions of tree-lines, fence-lines and hedges which separated one infinitesimal strip from another. But by the time I had learnt this fascination and learnt to love the vast skies which I allowed to take up three-quarters or more of my canvas, I wanted nothing else. Certainly not hills.

So when I came to Sheffield I had to begin another learning process, which I found difficult. I found a predominance of low clouds, and desired to brush them aside, as though a curtain was still half-drawn and the real day had not yet begun. I found the hills taking up too much room in the sacred sky, and I could not feel that the rocks were my friends.

But I saw a few of the paintings of Stanley Royle, and felt a little encouraged. The blues and greys of the sky were solid and darkish, and resonant, especially in combination with the partly-industrial pinks of cloud trails and smoke-trails. His moorland colours were also impressive and, for me, full of promise. I liked what he had done with the landscape, but I did not yet like the landscape itself. I saw only its surface, I think, and its surface oppressed me. I did my best; but my father was not encouraging. He rather disapproved of the move northwards (which was in any case beyond my control). I tried to be bright with him. 'There are painters up there, you know.' 'Oo?' said my father, in his most truculent h-dropping mood.

'Well, there's Stanley Royal for one.' 'Never 'eard of 'im', he said.

So I went to my Phaidon Companion to Art and Artists in the British Isles, which gives full and equal treatment to each region and is seemingly, therefore, not a London – and Home Counties-prejudiced compendium – and there he wasn't! 'He isn't there!' I was shocked. And my father smirked unbearably. Under 'Sheffield' there was a brief mention of one Alfred Stevens, the industrial designer, a Godfrey Sykes, a painter, and three kitchen-sink painters, Jack Smith, Derrick Greaves and George Fullard.

I was discouraged, and tended to think I had been trying to cheer myself up too much, thus seeing good things that weren't actually there. I didn't see a great deal more of Royle's work until the joint Exhibition in 1991, featuring the other artists of the area who had also gone to Canada and worked there. At that exhibition I saw his 'From Yorkshire Hills to Derbyshire Hills', and was most impressed. That sounds stuffy. But I felt inspired; and it finally convinced me of the pictorial possibilities, for myself as an artist, of this type of landscape. As I stood in front of the painting, I was struck again by something I had noticed before. The painting seemed indefinitely large. I felt impelled to measure it, which brought it down to earth. I said to myself, 'I often paint on that scale, but I can't get my work to look as large as that, not often, anyway'. So I began to formulate my rough rule: a successful landscape painting looks larger than it is – a failed landscape painting looks precisely the same size as the canvas it's painted on. (In fact, a failed one becomes the canvas, the paint, the cracks, the smell of the museum, the squeaky boots of the attendant, and so on.) A successful one creates its own space and its own world, and the medium becomes transparent, the revealer of that world.

I looked at the rest of the Royles, and enjoyed many of them, especially his scenes of Sheffield from various high vantage points. But 'From Yorkshire Hills to Derbyshire Hills' I kept going back to. It seemed to me then, and seems to me now, that it deserves to be alongside the best of Paul Nash and John Nash in the National and Tate Galleries . . . Oh, dear, what have I said? This is to imply that it is somehow wasted on Sheffield! No; Sheffield deserves to have it, and people should come up from London 'to look at the Royles'. That is how it should be.

But my thought of John and Paul Nash took me back again to my beginnings as a painter. At the age of sixteen I first saw Paul Nash's 'November Moon'. I thought: 'That's what I want to do. If I could just do something like that, just once, before I die.' I was saying, 'before I die' at sixteen! I then saw John Nash's ditch full of water, with an ivy clad tree standing at the end. Then I saw his various farmyards, usually in winter, with churned up mud, half melted snow, concrete and brick piggeries – things we would normally hurry past without a glance, our head tucked into the chest, our coat collar turned up high, our hands deep in the pockets.

But I understood why he had painted them, and felt the same fire beneath the surface. Later on, I came across T. S.

Eliot's lines in 'Little Gidding', which confirmed the passion:

The brief sun flames the ice, on pond and ditches,
In windless cold that is the heart's heat,
Reflecting in a watery mirror
A glare that is blindness in the early afternoon.

And glow more intense than blaze of branch, or brazier,
Stirs the dumb spirit: no wind, but pentecostal fire
In the dark time of the year.

Yes, that was it. It takes a fire within to respond to the fire that is locked inside prosaic things, dull winter things. Once that fire was burning in me, I could draw pigs in straw for hours on a winter's afternoon without feeling physically cold or spiritually shut out. I would go home rejoicing.

And that was also what happened to me, thanks partly to Stanley Royle, with the Yorkshire and Derbyshire landscape. The rocks became my friends. I became conscious of the fire within the rocks, and the fire within the rocks began to light the fire within myself. And once that is lit, there is fire everywhere.

And I knew that I had adjusted to the Yorkshire light in a visit to Essex last year on a bright blue March day, when an extraordinary pale white and blue light lit up Colchester. I said to my sister, 'Isn't this an extraordinarily light day?' And she said, 'No. Just normal.'

Bleaklow Moor, Sheffield

Troops' Concert

For an example of real courage in oddity I have to turn to Lance Corporal Lee, who was in the Signals Regiment in Germany where I was also stationed. I first came to know him because he came to our Education Office many times. (I was an Education Sergeant, taught various subjects, and helped to run a small branch library in the camp.) Corporal Lee used the library a good deal.

I found talking with him a little awkward. It was easy enough when he was merely seeking information about courses and exams. He had ambitions. He had taken his Army First Class exams, and now had his sights on the G.C.E. (This was in the 1950s, when millions of able people had understandably missed out on G.C.E.s, as the Secondary Modern system barely offered the opportunity.) But he also had literary ambitions, not only in terms of passing exams in literature, but in gaining a real appreciation of literature and, further, of trying his hand at writing it himself.

At this both my colleague Sergeant Gunn and myself gulped a little – meanly perhaps, but we certainly felt the need to be on our guard. This especially when Corporal Lee let it be known once that he wrote poetry, and might we be interested to look at it? We both smiled a bit grimly, Sgt. Gunn and I, and politely professed our ignorance in that sphere. We were lying, I'm afraid, and these days I feel ashamed of our meanness, and of copping out of the no doubt delicate and difficult task. It would not have killed us or him to have tried the poetry and possibly found it wanting. And possibly we might have discovered a genuine talent – or, of course, we might possibly have been confronted with one and failed to see it! It's probably too late now either to know, or to make amends.

We were put off, I'm afraid, by Corporal Lee's romantic demeanour. The 1950s was hardly the time for Shelleyan or Byronic stances, and the subsequent decades have not made such things any more possible. We were living then in the decade of The Angry Young Men. There was not a trace of anger in the serene Corporal Lee. He was slender, well-knit, if rather slight, and looking like Shelley in many ways, but with the Byronic dark hair and dark eyes (deep dark blue, I seem to remember). He seemed to have that rare combination of masculine and feminine qualities that, again, Shelley was described as having. His face was rather beautiful, in fact, but I'm afraid Sgt. Gunn and myself conspired to find him vain and ridiculous. Was this on account of the quietly glittering expression that he wore at all times? Or was it on account of the silk cravat that he always wore when in his very carefully selected civilian clothes? Or was it on account of his beautiful long eyelashes, like those of a girl, and seemingly cultivated?

I still had this suspicious view of him when I attended a Troops' Concert in our Camp towards the end of my Army service. I had given my friend Paul Zatz some editorial advice, at his request, for his own comic turn and Paul had just finished performing it, very creditably, at the actual Concert. He joined me at the back of the Hall to watch the rest of the show.

A great whooping jeer went up when Lance Corporal Lee walked onto the stage, in even fuller Byronic outfit than he affected at other times. He had managed to get hold of a sort of bottle-green jacket of the Romantic period, and had a folded silk cravat across his throat. In his hand was an old-fashioned small volume, with a gold binding.

'It is night' – the announcer solemnly said, to further whoops and catcalls. It *was* somewhat redundant, as it was night anyway.

Lance Corporal Lee walked soulfully and romantically across the boards, looking up at the rafters and the sky. Belches and jeers greeted his aspect once again.

'What shall I read tonight?' intoned Corporal Lee, in the full seething Victorian and almost girlish voice, fingering the volume and opening it at romantic random.

'Try reading Company Orders!' bellowed one wag 'About that silk neckpiece!'

Guffaws and shouts. Lee was unperturbed, his eyes literally sparkling and unashamedly yearning with their look of uplift and inspiration.

'Shall it be poetry of some great soul?' he went on.

'Or shall it be your own arsehole?' roared another wag, to further deafening and raucous cries. The Officers stirred a little at this, cast their eyes and heads round, with just a hint of warning.

Lee waited for the uproar to subside to some extent, and then pressed on through the murmurs and restlessness in his unperturbed way.

'Or shall it be some great work of drama, say, of Shakespeare, or of Jonson, or some fine playwright from a later day?'

'Only you can tell us, Lancey!' someone shouted, and there was again a fine commotion.

Corporal Lee waited for this to die down, and then, in the near-to-silence, paused a little before lifting up a flat defiant hand and intoning the single word 'Nay!'

This was just about fatal for the whole performance. The great whooping audience had wanted him off the stage from the second he had set foot on it; they had failed so far to drive him away, but this looked like the big chance.

'Nay?' someone shouted, with a great long question-mark in his voice.

'Nay, naaay, neigh, neigh, neigh' yelled the troops.

There were monstrous horsey neighing and whinnying sounds all round the hall, mingled with genuine amusement, not just jeering.

Lee waited once more for all this to die down. They had not shifted him. Was the man human? A kind of awe began to creep in.

He lifted a flat hand, and said it again.

'Nay!' he said.

'What!' came a collective incredulous roar 'He's done it again!'

'Heigh-ho neigh-ho, old Lancey' yelled a single voice, almost sadly, as though this were at last the end.

Corporal Lee waited. His hand was still lifted.

'Nay!' he said, for the third amazing time.

There was pandemonium. By now most people were not jeering, but laughing till they cried. It was turning into the most inspired comic performance of the whole evening. Some were in spasms, their feet lifted in the air and brought down onto the boards with great bumps and thumps. Others were drumming their feet on the floor with a regular rhythm. Others were draped over the chairs in front of them, seemingly sobbing. All embarrassment, and its defensive shell of whooping, had evaporated.

Corporal Lee was never in any hurry. He stood there benignly, like a perfect parent. By the time that this pandemonium had calmed down, the audience was quite simply spent. It had been reduced to the state of a child awaiting a bedtime story, and this was exactly what it got.

After his third and final 'Nay!' Lance Corporal Lee dropped his hand and opened another gilded book that lay on a little table a bit further back on the stage.

'Let us turn rather to a story old,
Of Night, and Winter-time, and Winter's cold.'

The audience, in hushed silence, sucked its collective thumb. Lance Corporal Lee then sat down at the comfy chair by the little table, and lit a candle. Then he took up a book, and read a passage from *A Christmas Carol*. He read, without any further interruption, and in beautiful clear cadenced and expressive tones, for about ten minutes.

When he had finished, he gently closed the book, he sat back in his chair and smiled gently at the audience. Then he stood up, and bowed. Light seemed to flow from him, out towards us, and up towards the heavens. His smile was radiant.

The audience stood up too. They stood up and they cheered and stamped and whistled, making possibly three times the noise, for certainly double the length of time, than on the occasions of jeering.

'The fickle mob' whispered Paul Zatz to me, as Lance Corporal Lee bowed again, and glided off the stage.

From 'Army Days' (from *Life Stories*)

The Cattle Run

A different sort of painfulness attended another contemplative walk of mine. I was strolling very gently in the wide flat pastures on the Suffolk side of the Stour, near Boxted Mill and to our Island Cottage. These pastures were split into a complex pattern of fields by thorn-hedges, wire fences, ditches and boundaries sometimes of small ash and oak trees. A herd of bullocks was grazing about a hundred yards away. They must have caught sight of my rapt expression, and decided that it was rather fatuous and absurd.

I had had a certain amount of experience of the countryside and its ways, and rationally I knew that bullocks were not dangerous. I had walked many times through fields of cows and bullocks, giving a little shout if a group of them became too curious or pressing in their attentions. But this time I caught sight of about twenty of them suddenly gathering in a throng and all looking at me, and then all running wildly about, with their tails in the air. And when the largest of them, who was way out at the front, suddenly stopped, and lowered his head, and began pawing the ground in the manner approved of in the Spanish bullring, and also with his tail in the air, twitching energetically, I decided that this was not the time for 'on the one hand this, and on the other hand that', but was the time, as in the case of the wasps' nest, for flight.

I turned round and saw it was a mere fifty yards to the loose wire fence from which I had entered the field. I soon reached this, and ducked under it. For good measure, I continued running, having once witnessed a whole herd of cows, on a hot thundery day, leap the barbed wire fence and go rampaging down the lane. In their present mood this herd could perhaps try the same thing. About two hundred yards away I could see my safe refuge, a good stout gate, and a pollarded oak, into which I could climb, if necessary. I reached here in an optimistic state.

The herd had neither jumped the wire, nor scrambled under it, but were returning to their point of origin. I sat on the gate and took breath, and smiled. I looked towards the road and the cottage. I had three more fields to negotiate, the last one rather large. Plenty of time, I said to myself, and 'downhill all the way' — metaphorically, of course, because the landscape was totally flat.

Then I looked round. My God, they were re-grouping. Their tails were still in the air, and they were milling about in an excited fashion in one spot. And suddenly they were all running in unison, streaming along towards a gap in the hedge that my eye now picked up, and that led into the field that I would have to cross. Surely they couldn't, at this distance of a quarter of a mile, have worked out my position, and know that that hedge-gap led towards me. But they had. And they had already reached the gap and were streaming through it before I had even got off the gate.

I jumped down from the gate and began to run across to my next point of safety, another two hundred yards away. And as I ran I shouted inwardly to those besotted creatures – 'Look here, you lot, I am a pacifist, I mean you no harm. I just came here for a harmless stroll!'

As I turned around to assess the situation, I seemed to pick up an answer from their kicking heels and waving tails. 'It's just because you're a pacifist that we enjoy chasing you. Don't we just know you're a pacifist!'

I reached my point of safety a good fifty yards in front of them, climbing another gate. The border was a fence plus a ditch full of water and reeds. They would hardly attempt to cross that. I breathed again on the other side of the gate.

But they had not given up. They immediately turned round and ran back towards the gap. They were going to find another gap and get through that into my safe field! They seemed full of an infinite cunning and malice. I saw them reach the new gap, go through it, and start swinging round to cut me off again.

I started to run once more, my breath beginning to be choked by a certain amount of fear. This time I shouted out loud to the empty air – 'I was at Swaffham, you ungrateful lot'. (At Swaffham in 1958 we Direct Action campaigners attempted to block the building of a Thor missile site, for which we received a two-week prison sentence.) 'I did it for you as much as for anyone!' I shouted, as I reached my next point of refuge, and threw myself on the ground, panting and choking.

After a few seconds I got up to look round. The cattle had not followed me into the previous field. They had aimed to cut me off in the very last field of all, the big one, and were already in it and streaming, not so much towards me as towards the fence by the road, so that I would be prevented from making my final escape. Their malice and cunning was beyond what I had already perceived.

This time I took one huge breath and sprinted harder than I have ever sprinted in my life. It was a good three hundred yards to the fence by the road.

'Remember Fylingdales!' I screamed aloud as I ran, like some demented clan Highlander rushing into battle. (Fylingdales was the Early Warning Station against which I had demonstrated in 1960, receiving one week's prison sentence in Armley Prison in Leeds.)

I reached the final fence only about twenty yards ahead of them. I leapt over it and threw myself to the ground, fetching great rasping breaths and cursing –'You bastards! You bastards! You bastards!' The cattle merely smirked, and frisked about.

Was it just another fancy of mine, or was it my employer John Bullough who passed by in a car as I lay there beating the ground? And did a flicker of something cross his face, as if to say –'Whatever is it now?' I could not be sure.

From 'My First Job' (from *Life Stories*)

Poetic Inspiration and Metaphysical Knowledge

Introduction

The poet and critic Kathleen Raine once said that most genuine poets have been Neoplatonists, even when they have known nothing about Neoplatonism. As a practising poet who believes in poetic inspiration, and as one who has been interested in Plotinus for over thirty years, I immediately felt in agreement with her. But the question facing me in this Paper is whether, when I really look into it, such a statement can be sustained, and, of course, whether it tells us useful things about both poetry and the metaphysics of Plotinus, and, more particularly, about what truth-claims can be made in either case.

Such an essay will necessarily be very personal, and I hope I will be forgiven for producing such a personal piece before knowing you, my audience, on a personal basis. I realise I am taking a risk, and that it will perhaps be difficult for you too, especially as I shall be claiming for myself experience of poetic inspiration, and the kind of mystical experience described by Plotinus – (which was the major source of his metaphysics). However, I promise I will not cause further embarrassment by using any of my own poems in illustration of my thesis.

I am using Plotinus as representative of metaphysics generally, partly because of his universality and huge influence on the three religious traditions of Judaic mysticism, Christian theology and mysticism, and some important currents in Islamic philosophy and mysticism. I am using him also because his metaphysics is based on personal experience, mystical and other, and though he was a system-builder, he was not guilty of the rather sterile system-building of later times. I am thinking of the systems of Descartes, Leibniz and Spinoza, which Kant rightly reacted against.

First let me say that I do not believe we should create a great divide between special experiences, such as poetic inspiration and mystical states, and the rest of our human experience. I am not presenting a disembodied mysticism. This is not because I believe there is nothing really special about these states after all. On the contrary, they are extraordinary states, with an intensity and fullness of content that can go on echoing in a person for years to come, and often for a whole lifetime. There may have been only one major experience, in the one mode or the other. Plotinus is reported by his younger disciple and pupil, Porphyry, to have had four experiences of mystical states in his lifetime, the later ones in the actual presence of Porphyry. This is not a great number of occasions, but because these states radiate and ramify and are tremendously fertile, in spite of their appearance of voidness, they have implications and workings-out in the rest of our human experience, resonating down the years.

But mystical experiences have these workings-out only if they are allowed to. There is unfortunately a rather decadent culture of mysticism, by which the experience of the Void is sought to be preserved at all costs. The mystical Void, and its 'unknowing' type of knowing, is severed from all lower modes of knowing, and the lower modes are cast to the flames forever. That is the 'hubris' of mysticism, its betrayal by human conceit, and is not my understanding of either mysticism or poetic inspiration. Nor was it that of Plotinus, nor the great mystics Eckhart and Boehme, nor indeed any of the classic mystics working within a philosophical or theological tradition. In the classical understandings, the mystical experience is made to do some work. It has a special energy and penetratingness which gives it relevance to the whole of the human framework and to other modes of knowledge. The great mystical theologian, the Pseudo-Dionysus, puts mysticism to work in this way, he never rests on the laurels of his inexpressible and uncategorisable experiences.

Poetic inspiration

Let me now turn to poetic inspiration, by considering the opening lines of a very fine poem by Edwin Muir, called 'The Transfiguration'. This poem is not only inspired, but it also explicitly records a visionary experience of a mystical kind, with a certain amount of actual theological comment. To be so philosophically explicit in poetry is often a mistake, but not so, I believe, in this instance. That being so, it relates to both aspects of my thesis, and should help to bring out, as we go on, significant similarities and differences.

So from the ground we felt that virtue branch
Through all our veins till we were whole, our wrists
As fresh and pure as water from a well,
Our hands made new to handle holy things,
The source of all our seeing rinsed and cleansed
Till earth and light and water entering there
Gave back to us the clear unfallen world.

Muir goes on to describe what he and his wife 'saw' in their visionary experience, how the world before their eyes was transfigured, and how the Christian hope of the restoration of all things was part of the experience. It was an unusual experience in being a joint one – he and his wife were travelling together, tired, but experiencing jointly this transforming, and knowing that they were both undergoing it at the same time. He goes on to say –

> We could have thrown our clothes away for lightness,
> But that even they, though sour and travel stained,
> Seemed, like our flesh, made of immortal substance.

Later in the poem the jointness of the experience is re-affirmed, with Christ also as a companion, through a kind of unsought reality-testing, their effect on others, which also tested its authenticity.

> And when we went into the town, he with us,
> The lurkers under doorways, murderers,
> With rags tied round their feet for silence, came
> Out of themselves to us and were with us,
> And those who hide within the labyrinth
> Of their own loneliness and greatness came,
> And those entangled in their own devices,
> The silent and the garrulous liars, all
> Stepped out of their dungeons and were free.

Clearly, a charismatic light shone through and around this couple for a while. People sensed something extraordinary about them, and were drawn to them, and sensed the possibility of a blessing from them. Equally clearly, it is not all to be taken literally – not every 'murderer' and 'lurker under doorways' in Vienna or wherever, 'came out to them'! The experience enabled the couple to have a vision of restoration, in which what is literally a possibility for the future has become a present reality. Strange things happen to time and tense in mystical states. But also people are indeed drawn to those who are in a state of vision of this kind. These things do happen from time to time, to quite ordinary people. Edwin Muir, unlike most poets, was also a good man and a modest one, and a good Christian, and he is not here boasting about his and his wife's charisma, but simply recording a moment of grace that was as extraordinary and surprising to himself and his wife as it was to the people around them.

The great founder of Quakerism, George Fox, records many such experiences in his 'Journal', of his own palpable transformation before people's eyes while he was speaking to them, and usually arguing with them, and even hectoring them. These powerful physical accompaniments of visionary states strongly affected Fox's thinking. Without at all denigrating the Soul, Fox came to think that a spiritual body, in St. Paul's sense, was even now operative in him and in others similarly inspired, and that such an experience would soon spread throughout England and transform society. This is one basis for the early social millenarianism of the Society of Friends.

William Blake in a state of poetic inspiration was apparently an awesome sight, a seemingly enlarged being, radiant, and almost frightening, given the actual content of some of his inspirations.

I want to quote the last few lines of Muir's poem before coming back later on to these physical concomitants of some states of inspiration. Muir is writing again about the hope of restoration. He considers the cross.

> . . . and the tormented wood
> Will cure its hurt and grow into a tree
> In a green springing corner of young Eden,
> And Judas damned take his long journey backward
> From darkness into light and be a child
> Beside his mother's knee, and the betrayal
> Be quite undone and never more be done.

These lines are really grand, and so moving that it is difficult to read them aloud without the voice breaking – but it needs the context and the momentum of the whole poem for the greatness of these lines to be felt, and I can only recommend, if you love and value poetry, that you read the poem in its entirety. Muir is putting on record his experience of what is often called the Eden-state (in Jungian terms, the Eden-archetype), but which I prefer to call the Sabbath vision, a future state of fulfilment which is both present and also out of Time altogether. Time and tense once again undergo strange transformations.

The connection between poetic and metaphysical-mystical
Leaving Muir's poem for a while, let me expound my general thesis. I believe that there is a congruence between poetic inspiration and the kind of metaphysical-mystical experience which leads to the metaphysical claims of Neoplatonism and allied schools. I am emphatically not seeking to validate the claims of metaphysical systems such as those of Spinoza, Leibniz, or Descartes, nor even those of Hegel and the Neo-Hegelians – though the Hegelian system comes close in certain respects to the Neoplatonic. If one reads Hegel's account of Platonists and Neoplatonists in his own 'History of Philosophy', one will find his debt to them gratefully acknowledged. But, in

the final analysis, his is a secularised version of Neoplatonism, and therefore a considerable deviation from it, even a betrayal.

In pursuance of my thesis I'd like to return to the opening lines of Muir's poem. It is unusual for even a poet of mystical experience to give, in the poem, the physical concomitants of the experience. It is good to have it expressed, and Muir is amazingly specific. Apart from sensations of lightness and radiance, there is the very specific reference to a something coursing through the veins, other than blood, and an even more specific and telling reference to a sensation in *the wrists*, 'as fresh and pure as water from a well'. The following line – 'Our hands made new to handle holy things' – thereby gains its true context and its force. It is concrete, sensuous, even while leading us to contemplate a most grand and heavenly vision.

It is my contention that the reason that inspired poets have been Neoplatonists, even without knowing it, is that the metaphysical expereinces of Plotinus at least, as the greatest of the Neoplatonists, are like the inspirational experiences of real poets. Those poets of the past who actually knew Plotinus's work, such as Spenser, and Sir John Davies and many of the Elizabethan poets in England, and Giordano Bruno and many others on the Continent, and later on Shelley and Coleridge, almost certainly gave their assent to it because they found that its actual structures, both at the mystical level of 'the One', and on levels below that, Plotinus's 'Nous' or Intelligible World, and below that the World-Soul or Anima Mundi in the Great Chain of Being corresponded to their own states of inspiration. Why else would a poet or an artist bother his head with philosophy, unless he could feel it spoke to him and was relevant to his craft and art? But many did.

It may well have been the reading of the plentiful vividly experiential passages in Plotinus which convinced poets he was a fellow-soul. But it is impossible really to separate Plotinus's account of his raw experiences from the mystical and other structures that he elicits from them. There is a more or less seamless transition from experience to the structure of interpretation. The experience radiates and ramifies naturally. Poets reading Plotinus might well have found that their own expressions, in the words and concepts and inner breathings of their poems, proceeded in much the same way from their original inspiration. Certainly I myself have found this to be so, in my own practice as a poet, and in my reading of Plotinus. He is a friend and an ally, one who really understands, and one who validates, in all sorts of ways, from his capacious sensitive beauty-seeing Spirit, and from his considerable analytic mind, the poetic insights that are vitally important to inspired poets.

Metaphysics and speculation

Metaphysics are usually thought of these days as 'mere speculation'. Kant has given metaphysics a bad name, though I am not convinced that he understood or had even read the by his time completely forgotten Neoplatonists. But even if he had read Plotinus, he would probably not have been much impressed. Kant did not believe we have a transcendent faculty for the immediate apprehension of transcendent truth, and Plotinus's demonstration of his own exercise of this faculty, in passage after passage of exhilarating insight and experience, would probably have left the later philosopher cold. He did not have ears to hear, and probably he had no ear for poetry either. And it is part of my thesis that if we have an ear for poetry, we will also have ears for what is called 'speculative metaphysics'.

The dominant meaning for the word 'speculation' has significantly changed in modern times, and Kant himself has played a major role in this change. Speculation now means guess-work, uncertainty, with a strong suggestion of self-indulgence and time-wasting. But for hundreds of years it meant direct insight, direct grasp of truth at a high level. Its literal basis was in a 'specula' or watch-tower, from which one could see very far, and see many things at once, and therefore see things in their true relation. It was not that the rational mind put many rational things together through seeing so many things at once. It was rather that being in a watch-tower state of mind, like gazing at a brilliant starry sky, can bring one into the presence of the spiritual realities which are above the rational. The experience of the spiritual level shows that spiritual reality is not to be determined by the criteria of a lower order. It also shows that the lower levels are in fact dependent orders of being, dependent on what is above them, while having at the same time their own autonomy and dignity.

Some of my own experiences

This again is not 'mere speculation', but can be actual experience. One can experience, not only something of the spiritual order itself, but the way in which it orders the other levels, the priorities of being. And I believe that both metaphysicians and inspired poets have this experience, for it is the foundation of much that they do. I know as a poet that the best work I have done has been accompanied by an experience in which my whole being is re-shaped. A re-structuring takes place, a 'something' that an ancient Greek would have called a god, a muse, a 'daimon', actually can take hold of the body and physically shake it into a fresh orientation. I then feel enfolded in one layer after another of the forces of being in what feels true ordering, like those Russian dolls, one within another. The lowest is not denigrated, but is in its place, and ready to do its work creatively in that place. The work of composition then proceeds with ease, and at an amazing pace, and with sureness of execution. Very little needs to be altered later, when my usual state of mind has supervened.

From my own experience too, I can say that exactly the same thing has happened a few times while reading mystical theologians. That is to say, the sense of re-ordering and a powerful re-shaping has taken place, even though on these occasions it was not given to me to be inspired to write a poem. Some 30 years ago I had decided to read Meister Eckhart properly instead of in snippets. I treated myself to the solid Pfeiffer edition in its English translation, and sat down to read the first of his Sermons, with the flamboyant title – 'This is Meister Eckhart, from whom God nothing hid.' This, and the next two that I read, are at the heart of his mysticism, and begin with the assertion of the need to gather up one's scattered being, to gather all one's faculties, senses, and mind, and feelings, and will, and to put them to rest in a silent place, and let the silence do its work.

I found that a rare energy was evoked in me, and this energy found its way to every part of my body, unlocking stiff joints, straightening my back, easing my head into a good position, and displaying itself in a curious fine sensitivity in my hands and fingers, and feet and toes. I even felt that the hair on my head was lifted up. (Those were the days when I had hair to be lifted up!)

At this point the door bell rang and I went downstairs to answer. A woman friend was there, and she immediately said 'You look extraordinary'. I said – 'Well, I feel extraordinary, and I'm afraid I need to go back to my work right now.' I hope I am not boasting, any more than Edwin Muir was. I was far less deserving of this special grace than he had been. However, these things happen, and one can only be grateful for them, and hope to be faithful and make proper use of them. I have only once spoken of this experience before now.

As I have said already, it is when I feel enfolded in these layers, in what seems like a true ordering, that at other times, when a poetic inspiration occurs, the poem energetically writes itself, almost merely making use of my hand and brain to put itself on the page. I then know, and other inspired poets know, that they inhabit the same universe as those mystics who do not disappear into the mystical void, but whose mysticism includes an energetic descent into the dependent orders of being. It is as though the energy of these creative mystics irradiates the dependent orders. Plotinus and Eckhart were precisely such mystics, being both mystics and constructive philosophers, using the sacred energy of the experience to do philosophical work in the lower orders. And I believe that that is the way philosophy in general should be done, a top-down approach complementing today's more common bottom-up method. If the top-down system takes too much control, it will try to dictate the realities of the empirical levels, and metaphysics in the past has often made this mistake. But there is still a use for the insights and energies of the higher order mind even in the empirical realm.

The Sabbath Vision in poetry and metaphysics
There is a body of poetry which gives expression to what I am calling the sabbath-vision. This sabbath-vision, though of course in different terminology, is found in Plotinus, in his descriptions of his experiences of 'the One', the highest of his three hypostases. (The others are the One-Many, or Nous, and the World Soul.) It is a state of sublime restfulness, and in speculative mysticism and in poetry alike one is enjoying the aspect of God as He is beyond His creation. I agree with Nicholas Berdyaev that we have a spiritual need of the non-creator God as well as of God as creator, and the creation itself, and ourselves as created beings. All these levels need to be honoured.

From the angle of the story, as myth of Creation, just as God rested on the seventh day, after the labours of Creation, so we envisage our rest after our business with all the levels of the universe is over, (which includes more than our struggles in this world, and takes in our developments and struggles in the next worlds, according to both Plotinus and the Christian Origen in the 3rd century.) And such rest can be had now, we can penetrate to that reality. There is nothing boring or monotonous about this sabbath. So long as it is not taken literally, or as an unvarying experience, it is inspiring. The Church's 'They rest from their labours' is an intensely moving statement in its appropriate context.

The value of its gift to poets is that others who have an ear for poetry can share in the experience, for it is usually mediated through the concrete occasions which are the ostensible material and content of the poetry. These concrete occasions are common currency, whereas many purely mystical writings are expressed in language and concepts which are often too remote from such occasions to communicate to many people. Usually only fellow mystics will understand, whereas the mystical in poetry can communicate beyond these. Great poetry comes closer to the world, and can lift up many others to the realm from which it has come.

Edwin Muir's poem was one of those that actually used some theological language in evoking the experience. Henry Vaughan and Traherne and Herbert will also do so, quite often. It does not necessarily spoil the poem or inhibit the experience. But it is usually better if an indirect approach is used, and of course nowadays it allays secular suspicion! Here is Wordsworth's sonnet 'Westminster Bridge':

Earth has not anything to show more fair:
Dull would he be of soul who could pass by
A sight so touching in its majesty:
This City now doth, like a garment, wear
The beauty of the morning; silent, bare,
Ships, towers, domes, theatres, and temples lie
Open unto the fields, and to the sky;
All bright and glittering in the smokeless air.
Never did sun more beautifully steep
In his first splendour, valley, rock, or hill;
Ne'er saw I, never felt, a calm so deep!
The river glideth at his own sweet will:
Dear God! the very houses seem asleep;
And all that mighty heart is lying still!

Wordsworth does not directly tell us but he conveys us to something higher and grander than London, the ostensible matter of the poem. It is not a trick — the poet himself may not fully know why he is feeling so strongly about his ostensible subject. He does not necessarily know that it *is* an ostensible subject, and more truly a symbol of a higher level. He is moved to give attention to it, perhaps quite naively, as the place where his vision will take its station, and he may be unwittingly, just as the reader is, conveyed to a mystical realm.

With Wordsworth this is especially true. He was an amazing visionary, sensing a mystical unity transcending the world, yet was at the same time dogged by a literal mind which insisted on pulling him down again and again. Some might think that his opening three lines are an example of this prosiness in Wordsworth, yet I would defend them strongly. They work, because they are full of the sense of the sublime something-or-other that at first absolutely overwhelms the poet as he stands on the bridge on a peaceful day, almost certainly a sabbath. The poet is first *smitten* into silence and inarticulacy by the power of the sight and his feelings, and then gradually the shaping powers give him his rhythm and his words and images, and the form and meter for the poem.

The first stumbling lines are a tribute to his having been overwhelmed by a vision, dumbness and a sense of wonder which, becoming articulate, is present throughout the poem. This higher vision is no denigration of London. There are bonds between great London at rest and the vision of high heaven. The glory of poetry is that both things are shown.

These sabbath-visions of poets, insofar as they are genuine inspirations, and not simply willed cerebral constructions, are of immense value. They take the poet and his or her audience beyond the reach of suffering, for the while. They are a palpable experience of a beyond-suffering state, of a unity and peace beyond creation. What we call hope is a pale image of the state they can sometimes communicate. Hope is what we practise when we can no longer directly dwell in this state, when the gate of this Eden has once again closed. There is a lesser poetry of hope, but the poetry of the sabbath-vision is sublime, is the pearl of great price. It can be occasioned by the most common things of our earthly experience, with the light of that sabbath shining through them. Dylan Thomas wrote in 'Fern Hill', talking of his childhood experiences on a farm –

And as I was green and carefree, famous among the
        barns
About the happy yard and singing as the farm was
        home,
In the sun that is young once only,
Time let me play and be
Golden in the mercy of his means,
And green and golden I was huntsman and herdsman,
        the calves
Sang to my horn, the foxes on the hills barked clear
        and cold,
And the sabbath rang slowly
In the pebbles of the holy streams.

Here we have that conjunction between the mystical realm and the ordinary things of earthly life that I was speaking of. It is a weekend on the farm, it is actually a Sunday, a Sabbath. 'The sabbath rang slowly In the pebbles of the holy streams' is a good description of the slow time of a Welsh Sunday in the old days, of a child's slow experience of time on any day, but especially when playing in clear streams on a quiet Sunday. And at one and the same time it manages to convey that the whole scene is suffused with the light of that mystical sabbath, beyond all pain and conflict, which is in our hearts, and which we are moved to tears by, when it is given inspired poetic expression. The child himself only half-knew it, even though he was in that special state of child-bliss. It is ourselves as adults in the retrospective experience who can come to know it in full, even while it is snatched from us a few moments later by the relentless and rapid movement of time, clock-time, adult-time.

Another of the virtues of great poetry is the slowing of time, the slowing down, so that we enter the child's experience of time, while having the adult capacity to see the vision through to its source, its transcendent ground. As adults we also know more fully the pains and the evils that the sabbath-vision offers refuge from. Yet we know, if it is fine poetry, and if we can respond to it, that it is not mere escapism. There is such a thing as pure escapism, and sometimes it is necessary for us. But escapism in literature does not move us to tears. Poetry can do so, because it offers consolation, and because it does not lie (even when poets are saying that they themselves are the greatest liars!) If it were a lie, we would soon know it. A false sound, a false rhythm, would soon tell us. But the true sound, the true unerring rhythm, tell us that the poem has indeed come from the land of the heart's desire. The poet has merely listened to what is being said there, and recorded it

Poetry as judgment

Sometimes we are aware, as the poet is, that we fail the vision even while experiencing it. When this feeling is dominant, the great vision is felt as a judgment on us, and a special sound and rhythm is in the poem. His poem, if it is a true one, is being shaped by the shaping forces from beyond him, but as his state is not itself mystical, there is not a sabbath-peace in the poem, but a certain bitterness, with its special clang and rhythm. But this itself can be bracing, and can convey to the reader more than is said. This is the level of Soul-struggle, and corresponds to Plotinus's third hypostasis, World Soul, in its relation to individual souls.

The poet is in a state of conflict, knowing his response to a situation is spiritually inadequate. Yet in inspiration, the spiritual healing forces are there, sounding through the conflict and bitterness. This happens in the Elizabethan Thomas Nashe's great poem at the time of a devastating and frightening plague, 'In Plague Time'. The third stanza goes:

> Beauty is but a flower
> Which wrinkles will devour;
> Brightness falls from the air,
> Queens have died young and fair,

Dust hath closed Helen's eye.

I am sick, I must die.

Lord, have mercy upon us.

There is also Thomas Campion's powerful 'Follow thy fair sun, unhappy shadow', and Shakespeare's bitter sonnet on lust, 'The expense of spirit in a waste of shame'. There is the bitterness of Blake's great lines from his 'Vala, Night the Third', with a great echoing of a higher something behind and above what is being stated:

What is the price of experience? do men buy it for a
    song?
Or wisdom for a dance in the street? No, it is bought
    with the price
Of all that a man hath, his wife, his children.
Wisdom is sold in the desolate market where none come
    to buy,
And in the withered field where the farmer plows for
    bread in vain.

It is an easy thing to triumph in the summer's sun
And in the vintage and to sing on the waggon loaded
    with corn.

It is an easy thing to talk of patience to the afflicted,
To speak the laws of prudence to the houseless
    wanderer,
To listen to the hungry raven's cry in wintry season
When the red blood is filled with wine and with the
    marrow of lambs ...

There are the dark sonnets of Hopkins, recording an intense struggle in a dark night of the spirit. These move us, because even in this extreme darkness the poet in his poem is being shaped by the forces of inspiration that belong to the realm of mystical peace. And less well-known, there is a remarkable wartime poem by Louis MacNeice, 'Prayer in Mid-passage', with that special emotional charge that war situations often generate, a prayer for help together with a penitence for sins and weaknesses. However, there is not room to quote this, as only in full does it show its qualities.

Another level of poetry and metaphysics

Apart from the many categories of genuine poetry below these levels I've been speaking of there is another major category. It is a reflection of activity and struggle within vastness. There is a sense of huge places, great 'halls'. I do not want to push too hard a point-by-point correspondence between the different levels of poetic inspiration and those in Plotinus's system. I am only too aware of the follies that are committed when system-making takes over.

Nevertheless, I do think that a correspondence exists between this poetry and Plotinus's occasional experiential descriptions of the realm of Nous, the One-Many, our true home as active beings. Blake said that 'Energy is eternal delight', and this level I am speaking of is the right context for the expression of that kind of energy. Blake at his best in the prophetic books gives the sense of it, a vast field for the exercise of enormous powers. It is the locus of active enjoyment, and is where most visionary poets will want to operate. Indeed it is sometimes said that Blake was not a mystic at all, but a visionary at this other level. Certainly there is very little sabbath peace in Blake's work. One will also find this particular energy in much of Victor Hugo's work, and of course in the cosmic Walt Whitman, who at his best is genius, and at his worst a platitudinous fool! We will also find it in several places in Shelley. Blake's long line, and Whitman's, and Hugo's, and Shelley's vertiginous sweep and speed, are all very appropriate for this level of reality. It is exhilarating to read inspired poetry of this sort.

Conclusion

To conclude, I would like to return to the tragic mode, in poetry and poetic drama, and to ask the question, why are these things not ultimately depressing. The answer to this question will give perhaps the most telling demonstration of how both poetry and metaphysics are truthful at a sublime level, and not mere subjectivism. If I say, because they are great poetry, that sounds both circular, and also a very glib answer. But if we try to identify what are the elements in the making of great poetry, the answer is not a glibness in the face of the world's suffering. When great tragic poetry is written, the poet is not only in the presence of the bitter feelings and tragic events, he is in the grip of the transcendent shaping forces, 'the gods', that have to be there if the poem is to be given its true shape and expression.

The presence of these higher forces, in the poet himself, and in his poem or drama, creates a resistance and a counter-reality that can qualify tragedy. The poetic communication of human dignity in the face of persecution and death qualifies tragedy, and such dignity only receives expression from a real source, the transcendent world in which it will be realised, and in which it is in a sense realised even now, if 'the gods' give the poet the sounds which convey it. So long as these forces, and these sounds and meanings are present, no tragic event can be felt as the absolute last word. The *beauty* of tragedy in art is precisely in the apposition of the eternal creative and healing forces against the actual tragic events and feelings recorded. If the poet is not inspired, he will not have access to the healing forces in his work. It will not do to name them, or to be consciously concerned with them, or to be passionate about them.. Sincerity does not in itself make poetry. It is a gift to be granted access to these powers for the expression of poetry. It is a rare gift. Our own culture is now more or less poetry-deaf, even more in its poets than in their audiences, but in cultures where poetry is still a force and widely appreciated, these uses of poetry are well understood, and the gift of inspiration is honoured.

In that fascinating play by Flecker called 'Hassan', written nearly 100 years ago, we are given an insight into a poetry-culture. The Caliph asks Hassan – 'When did you learn poetry, Hassan of my heart?' Hassan replies – 'In that great school, the Market of Bagdad. For thee, Master of the World, poetry is a princely diversion: but for us it was a deliverance from hell. Allah made poetry a cheap thing to buy and a simple thing to understand. He gave men dreams by night that they might learn to dream by day. Men who work hard have special need of these dreams. All the town of Bagdad is passionate for poetry, O Master.

Dost thou not know what great crowds gather to hear the epic of Antari sung in the streets at evening. I have seen cobblers weep and butchers bury their great faces in their hands!' The Caliph comments –'Ah, if there shall ever arise a nation whose people have forgotten poetry, or whose poets have forgotten the people, though they send their ships round Taprobane and their armies across the hills of Hindustan, though their city be greater than Babylon of old, though they mine a league into the earth or mount to the stars on wings – what of them?' Hassan comments – 'They will be a dark patch upon the world.'

Yet one might reasonably object that we trivialise real suffering and desperate situations when we say that terrible things in great poetry are not ultimately depressing. What does it matter whether they are or whether they are not? The question is, what is the fate of the desperate people, who are not likely to be reading poetry at the time?

Yet the really extraordinary thing is that desperate situations have stimulated numbers of people to remember poetry, or to try to get hold again of poems that have moved them, in the knowledge that it will help them. Others have even, under these pressures, written poetry, usually for the first and the last time in their lives, and often enough of surprising quality. Such was the case in the front line, in both world wars.

Even in the concentration camps people have witnessed to the healing power of poetry, to its capacity to inspire hope and endurance. Of course strong religious faith, with or without the adjunct of fine poetry, has been even more notable in its effect, but I mention poetry in these contexts because it has sometimes done what we would hardly expect it to do. Some who have not been able to make use of traditional religion, have nevertheless found its healing equivalent in poetry. Great poetry is for real situations, as it has in it the echo of a saving reality which people know as truth, not mere refuge.

Many of course are not helped or assuaged. A whole people can be conscious of a tragedy that has engulfed thousands, even millions, without consolation, without beauty, without hope. The world is more and more like that today. I do not wish to claim more for poetry, or for any power in this world, even religion itself, than it can deliver. There are many things that are not healed here, ever. Another world, and even some experience of oblivion, is needed. (The last line of Wilfred Owen's great poem 'Strange Meeting', set in another world, says 'Let us sleep now.') But still a real poet can speak for a people, a culture, as it tries to renew itself. The poet can have the power of speaking for all the voiceless ones who have gone down into 'death's dateless night' without help from the world. A people hears the voice of true poetry, and learns to grieve for the lost ones all over again, and learns perhaps that the dignity of those lost ones has not after all been lost. A tall order for poetry, but if there *is* a saving truth, a redeeming power, a preserving and healing power, anywhere beyond this astronomical universe, poetry makes only the claim to record it, and to communicate it truly.

Crossing France

A Moral Argument for Immortality

I would like to begin by quoting at some length from the Russian philosopher Berdyaev, who died some fifty years ago. This is the opening of the chapter called 'Immortality' from his book *The Divine and the Human*.

'The problem of immortality is fundamental, it is the chief problem of human life, and man only forgets it through superficiality and light-mindedness. Sometimes indeed he likes to persuade himself that he has forgotten it; he does not allow himself to think about the subject which is more important than anything else. The prayer that we may be granted the remembrance of death is a profound prayer, and the seriousness of life itself is conditioned by the remembrance of death, not one's own death but still more that of other people. All religions . . . have taken shape in relation to death. Man is a being who is faced by death throughout his whole life, and not only at his last hour. Man wages a double warfare; for life and for immortality. Death is something which is within life and not beyond it; it is the most stupendous of facts, one which borders upon the transcendent. Great suffering always raises the problem of death and immortality; but every experience which deepens life always raises the same question . . .'

I hope you enjoy, as I do, the forthrightness of that passage. Berdyaev is medicine for the Society of Friends, if only it would read him. He combines enormous learning and depth with the most courageous simplicity. He never tries to hide himself behind his learning, or to protect himself thereby from the possible scorn of his professional colleagues.

In the spirit of Berdyaev, my emphasis today will not be on the evidence for another world and life (though I believe such evidence exists) – but on the moral requirement that there be one. Part of my reason for taking this approach is the hope that fellow Quakers will be moved in their tenderest part, their moral consciences. If this begins to happen', prejudices about the whole question of the Soul and Immortality may begin to lose some of their force. And after that has occurred, Friends may begin to look, in an open-minded way, at the very interesting evidence.

One problem is that there are now many Quakers who no longer believe in God. For them my moral argument is of no use or relevance. If we don't believe in a God who has brought us into being in some way, and who cares for us, then we don't have to believe that the system of things is just, or will one day become just – though most Friends who reject both God and Immortality continue to hope for justice on earth. At the same time, and quite illogically, such Friends feel freed of a great burden in not having to think about the whole question of Immortality. It appears to simplify things considerably not to have to do so. Quite so, and it would simplify things even more to give up hoping for justice on earth, or peace, social harmony, and many other things that most Friends care for!

Most of us see immediately the terrible price that would have to be paid for such a drastic simplification. But what most current Friends don't see is the terrible price we are paying already for the drastic elimination of the Soul and Immortality from our concern and our spiritual life. For in the religious or Christian, and specifically the Quaker position, as traditionally understood, there most certainly is a moral requirement for another world, for the fulfilment of creation, because our sense of God's justice and love requires it. The question now is – Do we actually mean anything by what we say? To say, as many Quakers still do say – 'God is Love' – while at the same time strenuously denying another world, in which broken lives can heal, and begin to grow again, is a bit too much like saying – 'God is Love if you are lucky on earth.' It really is a bit too close to saying – 'God is Love if you are English and middle-class, and have lived somewhere in the Home Counties in the second half of the 20th century.'

Many Friends will reject this angrily. They may admit the social classification, while denying that this has spared them suffering. And they will be right, where this is true. But their arguments against the need for Immortality will nevertheless be strained and artificial, as I have found, and will continue to reflect this specific background and its gradually learnt assumptions. This is especially true when they argue that they don't ask for another life, that they are not interested in 'rewards and punishments', that they don't require 'the consolation' of another world, and so on. It is true even when they make the moral argument that a concern with another world morally distracts us from a proper concern with social and other conditions in this world. And my criticism is true especially when they maintain that God's Love for us isn't to be measured by any benefits conferred on us, and that the deep spiritual life is a mystery beyond any such practical or crude equations.

All this puts them on the moral high ground, as it is meant to do, and makes the rest of us seem rather grubby and calculating. The good Quaker, it is implied, must transcend the clamorous needs of the ego, and practise gratitude towards God for his or her life on earth, whatever it may be. But it is a simple fact, open to anyone's observation, that there are many lives in which the love of God has had no chance whatever to take root. Too many of us now, in our social concern for 'the wretched of the earth', brush aside a concern for the Soul and its fulfilment. Yet a social concern for a situation which is not quickly remediable, is not a remedy at all, and if there is no remedy for misery, we had better stop talking about knowing the Love of God. Berdyaev wrote in his autobiography *Dream and Reality* – 'Nothing is more pitiful than consolation derived from the idea of the progress of humanity, and the happiness of future generations. The consolation of eventual world-harmony as frequently offered to personality, always revolted me . . . Nothing 'general' can comfort the 'individual' man in his unhappy fate. Progress itself is acceptable only if it is effected, not alone for future generations, but for me, as well.'

Some people never seem to doubt the value and importance of what they will call 'the spiritual life in the Here and Now'. And yet, if there is no remedy for wasted and broken lives, and if it is not considered important to find one through another world, then it is surely frivolous to affirm the importance of the Here and Now, and the importance of 'spirituality.' Why is such a life important at all, and what makes such people so sure that God is listening? God will be listening to the broken and the lost, to the yearnings to which our Society has stopped listening. The 'spiritual life' of those who shut out those yearnings will be a merely self-referential circuit, composed of the illusion of reaching out and response. It is a game.

All that I've been saying might make it seem that the moral argument for Immortality is for some kind of compensation for unjust pain suffered on earth. But that is not my argument. The argument is that a creative loving God longs for the development, the flourishing and the return of all creation, for that is what the enterprise is about. The overarching spiritual idea is that whatever is created must fulfil its nature, and will not be thwarted. Essential to this idea is the understanding that nothing and no one reaches a full unfolding of itself in the limited conditions of this world. And the moral argument is therefore subordinate to a larger argument by which we are all unfinished beings, all needing other worlds and sets of conditions and experiences to complete and fulfil us.

Now of course the trouble may simply be that many people just can't believe in another world. Hostile Friends may drop their defensiveness and their pride about not needing another world, they may come to admit that a spirituality without another world is inadequate. 'There ought to be another world, but I just can't believe that there is.'

Here the role of evidence becomes crucial. Yet the moral concern remains relevant, for it becomes a question of how sincere we are in our desire to believe – that is, how much we are prepared to care. It consequently becomes a question of how much we are prepared to suffer inwardly for what we would like to see – of whether we are prepared to be turned inside out for it, as nothing less than that will bring us to any sort of conviction.

I t also becomes a question of who we will decide to venerate and follow within our Society. There is no disgrace whatever in being unable to believe in Immortality. If anything I have said has seemed to imply that there is, then I take it back with all my heart. What is truly shocking and disgraceful, however, is to see the few quiet people in our Society who do have such a serene conviction, marginalised and dishonoured. Their voice is silenced, and the really vociferous people in the Society are those who make it a point of pride not to believe in another world. They regard themselves as possessing thereby a 'superior' spirituality, and are determined to be leaders. These not only ignore the truly spiritual serene believers in another world, and try to lead where they should be following, but many will also crush and bully, so that the other people in our Meetings who want to talk about the Soul and Immortality are too terrified to do so. And these bullies in our Society regard their standpoint as 'reality', and 'seriousness', whereas they are precisely the people who are not fundamentally serious.

At this point I would like to go into a little theological history. The Christian Churches were always serious about the next world, but not always serious about God being Love. Both Protestants and Catholics believed, for much of their history, in the doctrine that God had predestined a few for Heaven and the rest for eternal Hell. Eastern Orthodoxy, to its great credit, never believed this, and the great theologian Origen, in the 3rd century, specifically taught universal salvation. But much of Origen was condemned by later Church Councils, and certainly in the Western Churches his universalist doctrine was buried and forgotten.

You may be surprised to know (for it is now never talked about in the Society) – that the Society of Friends holds a very special place in the revival of Origen's attitude and in the overthrow of the Calvinist predestination doctrine in which all mid-17th century Quakers without exception were brought up. Poor Isaac Penington was nearly driven out of his mind by it, as you can discover by reading the short account he gives of his life. The main contribution of the Quaker inspiration in the

17thcentury was precisely the re-discovery of the possibility of universal salvation, involving, it goes without saying, another world. And yet this is precisely the thing that is never talked about by modern Quakers. We have become the greatest betrayers of the very thing that our Society came into existence to proclaim. Among our modern Quaker scholars dealing with Quaker origins, it gets no mention whatever, apart from the work of the very fine H. G. Wood, who was an inspiring Warden of Woodbrooke for so many years. (Woodbrooke is now as though H. G. Wood had never been.)

To talk of universal salvation in the context of another world is to re-discover the phrase 'God is Love' in a truly meaningful sense. But in Quakerism today we have the melancholy situation of a universalism (in the sense of Truth from many sources and religions) without the salvation. That is to say, without the next world, or worlds, by which alone Universalism can make good sense. It is also ridiculous to claim to be 'open' to truths from all the other religions, and therefore to be universalist, while totally ignoring the concerns with another world which pretty well all the other religions talk about.

It is very strange. A deep inner life, which is what Quakerism still claims for itself, should make us aware both of the God within, and of the greatness of our own Souls, without which the reality of God cannot after all be grasped. In becoming aware of the greatness of the Soul, in apprehending God, one would expect the quiet conviction of its Immortality to follow naturally. Yet this is not happening in modern Quakerism. We could even be said to be in denial – and we need someone or something to shake us. Someone once said that the virtue of great preaching was that it wounded us with a sense of our own possible greatness. Perhaps we instead practise a spirituality of low self-esteem, and that we understand true humility to be the denial of our Soul and its Immortality.

Friends in the 17th century were turned inside out by their inner conflict from the Calvinism in which they were brought up. They could not rest until they had come to an inspired understanding of many things, of which universal salvation was the most important. It was a revolution. Quakers were persecuted for a generation, but predestination doctrines gradually died out. In the 18th century John Wesley thanked the Quakers for that.

It seems to me that nothing less than being turned inside out all over again is going to do for our Society if it is to grasp the importance of the issue being put forward here. And this is why I offer the moral argument to the tender conscience of our Society. It seems that only there, in a moral turmoil and struggle, are we so capable of wrestling with ourselves that we are in real danger of finding out the truth. We need first to look unflinchingly at the real tragedy of the world. Without for a moment taking our eyes off that, we need to ask ourselves if our current solutions are really solutions, and if we can really credit a spirituality that tries to manage without another world. The second step is to admit to the bankruptcy of previous approaches, whether frankly secular, or spuriously spiritual. We may then find ourselves for a long time in a painful limbo, having lost our previous certainties without having gained any true and life-giving certainty of the other world. Out of this pain, vision will begin to come, and when this begins to happen, actual evidence will become a useful supplement.

It may seem a miserable thing to focus on the world's tragedy. Yet if we never do, or do so without clear looking, without inner honesty, we will only succeed in being subliminally troubled by it, and in producing inauthentic and manic spiritualities. None of these give us any real hope, or give 'the wretched of the earth' any hope.

It is assumed almost without question that those working with such people should avoid all reference to the next world, and focus entirely on trying to improve conditions here and now. And of course in terms of words and concepts and talking and preaching, this is true. But in respect of the air that one brings into such endeavours, and in respect of one's inner spiritual attitude, it is the reverse of the truth. It is joy, and the attractiveness of joy, that is the thing. Once again, people with no belief in another world can carry this joy, but it is the air of heaven, if it is there, that the hopeless will sense. And a truly spiritual person will radiate the joy of heaven, and will be loved for this very thing among the destitute.

Also, such an air and attitude is a great leveller. While we, the comfortable, try to help the wretched, there is in fact a gulf that will never be bridged so long as we believe in nothing but this world. For the fact is that we are fortunate and privileged in terms of the only reality that is deemed to exist. And in that situation and relationship, the supreme reality of this world feels oppressive to the poverty-stricken. It is a kind of imperialism. And that privilege will remain, no matter what we do or achieve (unless we adopt a voluntary poverty, permanently, on the same level as those we are trying to help).

But to share with the unfortunate our hope of heaven and our need of heaven is to qualify our own judgment of the value of the material world in a way that brings us together. Without this shared hope we remain the 'them' who have reality, because we have money and goods and security, while they remain the 'us' who are powerless and have failed to experience reality. For if this world is the only world, then it is reality, and it is an unmitigated pain not to have had it and enjoyed it.

But if there are the heavens, then for both of us the heavens are the greater reality, and in affirming that we also reach out to our common humanity. And once this bond is made, in the things that are eternal, we can surely work more freely and surely together in setting about the problems of poverty, and making things more comfortable and sane and secure – certainly everyone's birthright, without any doubt. It is only a comfortable right-wing attitude of the old and totally unacceptable kind that asks people to be satisfied in their poverty, because there is another world. I am a lifelong Socialist, and I have no truck at all with such an outlook, and it is not this view that I am propounding. I am wanting to break altogether with the terms in which the matter has been put in the liberal Western world for so long.

For it is all very well to criticise those right-wing religionists who are happy to fob off the poor with the hopes of heaven. That is the easy part, which we have done with some glee. It is not even an issue any more It is old hat. The hard part is to look at ourselves as a Religious Society, and specifically at our recent failure in this crucial area of the Soul and its aspirations. We are in no such superior position that we can afford to make fun of what are after all easy targets. We need seriously to look to ourselves, at our own terrible deficiencies and smugness, our smug contentment with the things of this world, and our smug conviction that we have devised and practise a 'spirituality' that is an adequate response to our sense of the divine, and that provides, in a totally secular framework, some kind of 'spiritual' answer to everything, and all the world's problems.

The simple fact is that we have, as a Society, and as individuals, enjoyed inordinate wealth and security for far too long, and our secular so-called spirituality is a reflection of that. There is actually not much hope for us at all, if the truth be known, unless we realise with horror our own smugness, and then set about praying deeply for a cure for it, and for a new vision- the vision of those heavens in which all creation will be gathered up.

There is in American Indian spirituality the notion of 'Crying for a Vision'. People are granted a vision by sighing and crying for it And yet there is the frank recognition that some are granted the vision, while others are not. Those who are not will venerate those who have received it, while meanwhile their state of sighing and longing goes on. We just cannot say how long we might remain in the limbo of uncertainty about the existence of the other world, or worlds. But it doesn't matter if we are there for the rest of our lives. We might cure it by a resort to Spiritualism (which should always be available as a part of our religious life), in which we receive a clear message. On the other hand, we may not receive a message at all, or it may be so blurred that it cannot help us.

This does not mean that we should cease to sigh and groan for the other world, for such sighs and groans open our spirit and help the spirits of others in ways it is impossible to specify, but which are very real. This is a real stage in a real spiritual life, unlike much current spirituality which is based on the absolute and dogmatic certainty that there is no other world, and that we must base our orientation towards God on practices and attitudes that do not entail it. And going with that , there is a determination to suppress the voices of those who feel and think differently on this most important of all issues.

The person who is sighing and groaning for some glimpse of the other world is facing in the right direction, and if a whole Meeting were allowed to face this way what a difference there would be. Isn't it time we began to try this? I hope that all that I have said in this talk will encourage those who want such a change in our Meetings to find the courage to ask for it. For as Keats wrote in his 'Hyperion' (in which an angelic figure is standing at some high point on the steps of another world):

None shall usurp this height
But those to whom the miseries of this world
Are really miseries, and will not let them rest.

(Adapted and enlarged from a talk given to Quaker Fellowship of Afterlife Studies 2002 and to Leiston Quaker Meeting 2003.)

Mystical Sabbath and Heavenly Work

I am a Quaker, and also a recent member of the Swedenborg Society. I am not as well versed in Swedenborg's writings as I would like to be, but one aspect that struck me as long as forty years ago was Swedenborg's statement 'The Kingdom of Heaven is a kingdom of Uses'. I liked this, and still do, and it is connected for me with William Blake's 'Energy is eternal delight', and with the 'tremendous labours' of Blake's central figure, Los, with his furnace and hammer and anvil, a symbol of the great divine-human works of Imagination (Blake's term), that engage us in this world and the heavenly worlds.

Also, I had an occasional companion in those days, Frank Rose, at present a Swedenborgian minister in Arizona. Frank had stayed earlier on as a lodger at my parents' house in Colchester for a year or so, when I was about 14. My mother introduced him to me at the tea-table on his first day at our house, and said 'Mr Rose is studying theology.' I was still a bit of a Just William, I'm afraid, and I immediately said – 'What on earth is theology?' 'Oh David! said my mother and Mr Rose in the same shocked breath; and then they tried to tell me a little of what it was.

I must have been an incipient modern Quaker even in those days (I am not a birthright Quaker), for even after their explanation I was as baffled as before. I did not see how there could be any such thing as theology. And to an extent this attitude remained with me a few years later, when I enjoyed the occasional genial and scintillating discourses of Frank, sometimes as we travelled in a train to London. I had already discovered William Blake, but did not 'theologise' him, nor at that time did I take his heavenly worlds to be anything more than metaphors for our human experiences on earth. (This outlook is very common today, and continues to distort the work of scholars on Blake). However I was fascinated by Frank's confidence in the human ability to communicate something of the reality of God and of the heavens by mere speech, and by *diagrams*. For Frank would draw diagrams for me, on the spot, illustrating points concerning Divine Wisdom, and other matters. I was both amazed, and somehow appalled, at these illustrations.

Perhaps it was Frank's American innocence and freshness, if I dare postulate such a thing, coming up against my Old World tiredness and melancholia. Frank was a continuous bubbling spring of pure and elaborate expressiveness, his face and his eyes lit up and mobile, and his large hands and long fingers searching out, and finding, the most curious shapes and motions to accompany his meanings. I remember Frank as also double-jointed, and the ability to bend his fingers *both ways* added enormously to the effect.

This may sound trivial, but it was not. His expressiveness, his confidence and energy, his permanent high spirits on a high plane, his total lack of pomposity or heaviness, and at the same time his thorough commitment to what he was doing and believing arid experiencing – all this came over to me as a living illustration of Swedenborg's Doctrine of Uses.

However, what he also came up against in me was what I will call my 'Sabbath mysticism'. I had experienced by that time certain things of a mystical nature, rather shallow rooted to be sure, but having enough intensity to be contributing an important current to my life. Descriptions of 'the negative way' – in Eckhart, or in the Hindu Upanishads, made complete sense to me, and I could not see that anything more was required. To talk of the heavenly worlds as something real and additional to this world, seemed to my mysticism unnecessary, almost a sacrilegious breaking of what I then thought was the unity of all things. (And this unfortunately, is too often what has happened to mysticism in our century.) I felt that Swedenborg was a visionary in a rather ambiguous sense, of worlds whose 'objective' reality I did not then need, and that he was, in any case, not a mystic. I probably supposed a connection between his 'lack' of mysticism, and his 'mistaken' belief in the objectivity of the heavens.

I've called it a 'Sabbath mysticism', by which I mean the realm of the most supreme restfulness, a kind of seventh day rest after the labours of creation. Just as God rested then, in the literal aspect of the story, so we can rest in Him, and in doing so, somehow get beyond both Creation and the Creator-God. It is as though we can use our own faculty for the infinite to peer into that mystery of God's being that has nothing to do with the making of worlds. Eckhart described this as 'the Godhead', higher than 'God'. It is where 'God does no work'. Such a mysticism is not sufficiently indicated by the mystical unity of all things. It is more than that, it is a point of rest, and a boundary of darkness, beyond which our access is limited. Though it is beyond us, we have a spiritual need for it.

For the slaves of the old plantations, the greatest heavenly dream was of rest, their songs were often about rest, and simple though they are, they have a tinge of this mystical quality. In my own personal history, to find spontaneously, and as a gift from God, this great mystical Sabbath rest, this pure still Nothing, as Eckhart would call it, was a miraculous release from my own emotional turbulence and turmoil.

I do not repudiate those mystical states now, but only the false interpretations that I at first put on them. I have been a painter for some thirty years, and most people see that my best works are those that express this 'mystical Sabbath' – for insance a huge flat rolled East Anglian pinkish field, in October, that Sabbath of all months, stretching out into a blue distance, and resting under a vast and peaceful sky. I make these paintings anything from four feet to six feet in length, and it is still profoundly satisfying to me to conceive and to carry out these expressions.

It was precisely through expressiveness, in fact, that I began to change my attitudes, and to come closer to good old Frank Rose and to Swedenborg. For I found that these mystical states in their occasionally prolonged peacefulness, resulted eventually in a build-up of a very special energy, waiting to be released for creative purposes. I was ready or becoming ready for some creative Uses. I became a poet, at about the same time that my painting gradually became able to express the Sabbath rest, and other aspects of existence. Later on I began to feel that this energy should also be expressed through thought, more particularly , theological thought. I began to believe that theology could, after all be done – and by this I mean, not by me but by great theologians of the past, whose works now drew me powerfully.

I never spoke with an angel, or saw an angel, or saw any special vision of. that kind. What I did experience were glimpses of what I believe is the higher structure of the worlds, by a sort of intuition, and corresponding to changes of the *positioning*, as it were, of my own faculties and powers, as the energies re-shaped me and possibilities of expressiveness were growing in me. It was not much, but it was enough to bring me out of a rather quietist (and secular) mysticism common in Quakerism, and into a real appreciation of the heavenly worlds, and an enjoyment of the prospect of energetic creativeness and development beyond physical death, as described by Swedenborg.

It has also brought me out of the furthest margins of Quakerism, for most modern Quakers do not acknowledge a need for heaven, and the 'energy' of 'eternal delight' in the heavenly worlds. If they did, there would be nothing better in the world, as a form of worship, than the mainly silent Quaker Meeting, that Sabbath-point out of which the amazing heavenly energies would emerge. We need active human fellowship, both in this world and the next, though our inmost part may be that infinite spark that conjoins with the mystical God, God in his aspect of darkness and of rest. It is not necessarily private, we can meet others there at their greatest depth. We need to be double jointed in our spiritual apprehendings.

(From *Things Heard and Seen* (newsletter of the Swedenborg Society) Vol 7 (Spring 2002): http://www.swedenborg.org.uk/.)